10/14

BOOKSTART
PLUS

Southwark
Council

**DULWICH WOOD
CHILDREN'S CENTRE**
Kingswood House
London SE21 8QR

Please return/renew this item
by the last date shown.
Books may also be renewed by
phone and Internet.

Coping
with
Two

A stress-free guide to managing a
new baby when you have another child

Simone Cave and
Dr Caroline Fertleman

HAY HOUSE

Australia • Canada • Hong Kong • India
South Africa • United Kingdom • United States

First published and distributed in the United Kingdom by:
Hay House UK Ltd, Astley House, 33 Notting Hill Gate, London W11 3JQ
Tel: +44 (0)20 3675 2450; Fax: +44 (0)20 3675 2451
www.hayhouse.co.uk

Published and distributed in the United States of America by:
Hay House, Inc., PO Box 5100, Carlsbad, CA 92018-5100.
Tel.: (1) 760 431 7695 or (800) 654 5126; Fax: (1) 760 431 6948 or (800) 650 5115.
www.hayhouse.com

Published and distributed in Australia by:
Hay House Australia Ltd, 18/36 Ralph St, Alexandria NSW 2015.
Tel.: (61) 2 9669 4299; Fax: (61) 2 9669 4144.
www.hayhouse.com.au

Published and distributed in the Republic of South Africa by:
Hay House SA (Pty), Ltd, PO Box 990, Witkoppen 2068.
Tel./Fax: (27) 11 467 8904. www.hayhouse.co.za

Published and distributed in India by:
Hay House Publishers India, Muskaan Complex, Plot No.3, B-2,
Vasant Kunj, New Delhi – 110 070. Tel.: (91) 11 4176 1620; Fax: (91) 11 4176 1630.
www.hayhouse.co.in

Distributed in Canada by:
Raincoast, 9050 Shaughnessy St, Vancouver, BC V6P 6E5.
Tel.: (1) 604 323 7100; Fax: (1) 604 323 2600

A catalogue record for this book is available from the British Library.

ISBN: 978-1-84850-812-5

Printed and bound in Great Britain by TJ International, Padstow, Cornwall.

To Lewis, Douglas, Natalie, Harry, Tobias and Betsy

CONTENTS

Introduction   ix

Chapter 1 Early Pregnancy   1

Chapter 2 The Final Weeks and Days Before the Birth   17

Chapter 3 Bringing Your Baby Home   31

Chapter 4 The First Week   39

Chapter 5 The First Day on Your Own   51

Chapter 6 The Early Weeks: 1–6   71

Chapter 7 The Early Weeks: 6–12   87

Chapter 8 Months 3–6   99

Chapter 9 Months 6–12   113

Chapter 10 The Second Year and Beyond …   133

Chapter 11 Sibling Rivalry   151

Chapter 12 Illness and Injury   173

Chapter 13 Age Gaps   189

Chapter 14 Are You Going to Have Any More?   195

Chapter 15 Routine   201

Resources   211

Acknowledgements   213

Index   215

Troubleshooting Index   223

INTRODUCTION

Being pregnant with a second baby is daunting for most mums. You may well be struggling along with your first child, and soon you'll have to cope with another one. How does anyone manage with two or more children? Surely it's an impossible task that can only lead to insanity and chaos?

But look around. You'll see families of two, three or more children that are busy, happy and content – with lots of laughter and joy along with the usual everyday squabbles. The truth is, having two or more children isn't the nightmare that some parents fear – while it can be busy and stressful, the pleasures and rewards of family life far exceed the daily challenges you'll face.

Mothers of such families somehow manage to get their children fed, bathed and put to bed day in and day out, not to mention organizing the cooking, laundry and family social life. Just how do they do it?

Well, it's not rocket science – in fact, in most cases it's just down to experience. In *Coping with Two* we give you all the necessary tips, techniques and strategies so that you can manage a new baby and another child right from the start. We explain how to organize everything from bathtime and bedtime to leaving the house.

You'll become so proficient that within a couple of months you'll be asking yourself, 'How did I ever find looking after one child difficult?' Because now, whenever you're with just one of your children, you'll find it a doddle.

We recognize that things often don't go to plan when you have small children, which is why we include troubleshooting sections throughout the book to help you through those inevitable moments when it all kicks off. And we've also included a troubleshooting index so that you can identify key issues that your family is facing and find potential solutions quickly and easily.

Like our previous books, we've written this in an accessible dip-in-and-out style, and given masses of reassurance throughout. We're not trying to tell you what to do, but just give you options and ideas you can draw from – ultimately, you know what works best for you and your family.

Beginning with early pregnancy and how to tell your eldest about the baby, the book takes you right through to when your children are old enough to argue and fight, and to when you may be thinking about baby number three … or not.

Throughout the book we've referred to the baby as 'she', and the toddler or older child as 'he' in order to maintain consistency and keep the book easy to follow, no matter which part you're reading. Obviously you can swap this around as appropriate, but the meanings and advice will stay the same.

WHO IS THE BOOK FOR?

There's a lot of focus on mum throughout the book; she even has her own section in the first 10 chapters. We've chosen to do this, rather than having a section for mum and dad, because mum is the one giving birth – the first two chapters of the book are on pregnancy and birth, and we talk about post-birth issues in subsequent chapters. Also, in the majority of cases it is mum who goes on maternity leave and is the one in sole charge of the children, particularly in the early months.

We've included tips on breastfeeding in each of the 'Mum' sections because so many women find breastfeeding especially challenging when they've got another child – we wanted to give as much support as possible. We've put less emphasis on bottle-feeding simply because this is more straightforward than breastfeeding if you have another child. But bottle-feeders could still glance through the section for tips on growth spurts and also keeping their toddler amused while they feed the baby.

We've written the book assuming that just one person will be doing the bulk of the childcare, likely in many cases to be mum. However, this doesn't mean that dads can't read the book and get just as much out of it. They will certainly benefit from being up to speed on many of the strategies outlined in this book, as they will no doubt be looking after the children on their own on occasions, especially at the weekend. Grandparents, too, will benefit from the book if they find themselves having to look after two children once mum goes back to work.

We felt it was important to give strategies enabling either mum, dad or another carer to cope alone. Then any help you happen to get is a bonus, and when extra childcare isn't an option you'll still be able to manage.

GETTING THE MOST FROM *COPING WITH TWO*

The first 10 chapters span from before your baby is born to 'the second year and beyond'. We take you chronologically through the early weeks and months, guiding you through the new baby chaos when you've got a toddler or older child in tow.

Each chapter has different subheadings including 'Baby', 'Toddler' and 'Child'. In the 'Baby' sections we talk in detail about your baby's basic needs in the early weeks and months, as well as reminding you about various developmental milestones and how these will impact on your eldest. Although you'll find looking after a baby much easier than first time around, all babies are different so you probably won't be a baby expert in everything. We have tried to second-guess such instances, for example if you have to deal with colic for the first time. We have also tried to anticipate specific difficulties you may encounter with a new baby as a second-time mum.

In Chapter 10 we continue to use the 'Baby' heading despite your 'baby' being at least a year old and probably starting to walk and talk. But we felt that by keeping to the same heading for your youngest child, it makes the book easier to navigate.

The 'Toddler' heading refers to children under 3 who aren't yet at nursery. The 'Child' section refers to children who are 3 or older and may be at part-time nursery, full-time nursery or school. This enables you to select the section – either 'Toddler' or 'Child' – that is most relevant to your child's age and stage. You may find that your 'toddler' grows into a 'child' and starts school as you work your way through the book. If this is the case, we suggest that you read both sections while your eldest makes this transition.

In Chapters 1 to 10 we've also included a 'Housekeeping' section. This may sound a little old-fashioned, but we know from experience that although you can just about get away with running a haphazard household when you've got one child, when you have two you need to be super-organized. So this section aims to help you become the sort of person who has a freezer full of home-cooked meals and an organized laundry system – with plenty of cheating and shortcuts along the way.

One of the most important chapters in the book is 'The First Day on Your Own', Chapter 5. This is the day that many new mums dread, as they wonder how they will cope by themselves. So we decided to devote an entire chapter to the subject, taking you hour by hour through the day. This simple guide will ensure that you're not still in your pyjamas at 2 p.m. with the breakfast stuff not yet cleared away. And that you can find time to check your emails and have a cup of tea – sitting down! We hope that this chapter will not only get you through the day, but stop you dreading it, too.

We've also included a chapter on sibling rivalry, explaining why siblings fight, how to cope when a fight breaks out and teaching your children to get along. We suggest you read this as soon as you feel any stirrings of favouritism towards one of your children, and also from when your youngest is 16 months and old enough to provoke your eldest.

We've included a chapter on illness which you can read as soon as one of your children catches a cold – with two children there are new issues to consider including how to prevent the spread of bugs and managing the healthy child's jealous feelings towards their sick sibling.

And, looking to the future, we've written chapters on different age gaps, as well as a chapter about going on to have more than two children.

Even when you've finished this book, we hope that you will continue to refer to the information in Chapter 15 which covers sleep and feeding patterns for the years to come. These tell you how much sleep your children should be getting from when they are a week old to when they are 18. Likewise with feeding, the information in Chapter 15 takes you from the first week through to weaning and beyond. This information should prove to be invaluable in helping you devise a family timetable and routine that meets each of your children's needs.

Most importantly, we want this book to give you both practical help and comfort along the bumpy journey of coping with two young children so that you can relax a little, enjoy your growing family and have fun.

CHAPTER 1
Early Pregnancy

During your first pregnancy you may well have pampered yourself, getting plenty of rest and perhaps even treating yourself to the occasional mum-to-be massage or two. But now that you've already got a child, it's probably a rather different story.

As well as coping with the physical aspects of being pregnant second time around, you'll also have to deal with the emotional issues of telling your first child about the baby. In fact, you'll probably spend much of this pregnancy obsessing about how your eldest will react to the baby once it arrives. You may question your own feelings – will you ever love this baby as much as your eldest? (The answer is that of course you will.) And then there are the logistical matters such as organizing childcare, and taking a toddler to antenatal appointments.

So it's a busy emotional time, and this can be exacerbated by the fact that when you announce that you're pregnant again, people won't react with the same excitement as last time. As far as they're concerned, you've done it before, you seem to be coping, so what's the big deal?

Well it *is* a big deal. Having two children is a wonderful experience – you'll not only have created two individuals, you will also have set in motion the relationship they will have with each other. And watching your children being kind and loving with each other has to be one of the best experiences a parent can ever have. Yes, it's normal for siblings to punch, kick and compete (more on that later), but it's also normal for them to love each other very deeply.

MUM

You'll probably find that you are more tired with this pregnancy than with your first. This is partly because you'll be a bit older than last time, which can take its toll – especially if you're approaching 40, or older. You'll also be a lot busier looking after child number one, and you may well have the odd disturbed night. So it goes without saying that you need to get plenty of rest – early nights may be more practical than afternoon naps, especially if your child isn't yet at full-time nursery or school, or if you are back at work.

A particular plus-side to resting is that it seems to help with morning sickness, which can be very tough with young children, especially when it comes to feeding them. The sticky chaos of high-chair meals, or even just cooking fish fingers, can be hell if you're feeling nauseous.

Ideally, get some help around mealtimes. But on the days when you are on your own and feeling sick, we suggest that you resort to toddler ready meals that you just have to microwave, or easy-to-prepare food that doesn't smell too strongly, for example ready-cooked chicken slices, frozen peas and pasta. A jar of baby food is another good emergency meal if your child is still very young (it will smell less if you don't heat it). One advantage of morning sickness is that you'll be beyond caring whether your child finishes his meal, or indeed eats very much at all, and this can help resolve any fussy eating issues – see the troubleshooting on page 14.

The tiredness of early pregnancy will force you to play with your child in a different way. Rather than chase around energetically, you'll have to spend more quiet time – cuddling, reading stories or doing jigsaws together – all good bonding activities.

You'll find that you start to show earlier than with your first pregnancy because your abdominal muscles will be more lax. So even in the first 3 months, any bloating caused by the pregnancy hormone progesterone will be more pronounced than previously. And as your pregnancy progresses you may well look bigger than last time. You'll also feel the baby kicking much earlier.

Preparing for Birth

Assuming your pregnancy is uncomplicated, you will have fewer antenatal appointments for your second baby than for your first. You'll have seven appointments this time whereas you would have had at least 10 for your first baby. If during your pregnancy you have any concerns, you can book an extra appointment with your midwife. It's perfectly normal to worry from time to time about the birth, but hopefully you'll be less anxious than your first time.

Depending on where you live, it may be possible to have your antenatal appointments at home. This is more convenient, especially now you have another child, so it's always worth asking.

If You Had a Traumatic Birth Last Time

You may well be even more frightened than before. Try to pinpoint what you are most afraid of happening and talk to your midwife about it, perhaps getting her to talk you through your birth notes from last time. Your midwife should be able to put your mind at rest. It may also be worth reading up on hypno-birthing or listening to a DVD. The very positive attitude of hypno-birth experts may help you to feel more confident and relaxed about labour even if you don't go the whole way and get into a hypnotic state on the day.

If You Had a Caesarean Last Time

It may still be possible to have a vaginal birth this time. While the statistics are against you – only 33 per cent of women have a vaginal birth after a

Caesarean – a lot depends on why you had a Caesarean last time. If your pelvis is small and your baby got stuck then of course you're more than likely to have another Caesarean this time. But if your baby was breech or you had a low-lying placenta, and these aren't affecting you this time, then a vaginal birth is more likely.

During labour you will be put on continuous fetal monitoring to detect any problems with the baby – there is a tiny chance that your scar may rupture during labour, and this has to be picked up quickly. Your midwife will also be checking that your labour is progressing fast enough and that you are not pushing for more than about an hour, which can put a strain on your scar.

Of course there's a chance that you'll end up having another emergency Caesarean, which can be very disappointing. One of the best ways of consoling yourself in such a situation is to understand why – so talk to your midwife about the reasons you may end up with another Caesarean. And remember, some women go on to have a vaginal birth after two Caesareans, so it may not be over just yet …

NATURAL BIRTH

Our big tip is to do your absolute best to avoid an epidural, as this will help keep your labour swift – epidurals can slow labour down, and this makes complications more likely. If you do end up needing one, though, don't feel guilty, just be thankful for modern medicine.

BABY

Second babies are often bigger. This can be because placental function and blood flow is more efficient, and sometimes it is simply down to genetics. But it's certainly not always the case that subsequent babies are bigger.

When it comes to having your scan, you'll need to decide whether to take your eldest child with you. It can be interesting for your child to see a picture of the baby in mummy's tummy, and this will make the whole thing seem a bit more real. But remember that the purpose of the scan is to look for abnormalities. Although statistically this is unlikely, do think through how you would cope with bad news if your older child were present at the scan.

The other decision you'll have to make is whether to find out the sex of your baby. This is a very personal decision but it's basically down to whether you like surprises or whether you like to plan. Bear in mind that if you have a strong preference as to whether you want a boy or a girl, you'll probably cope with the disappointment of not getting what you want far better when you're holding your new baby in your arms. Lots of parents have been bitterly disappointed when told the sex of their baby at the scan.

Most parents hope for 'one of each'. But if you have two boys or two girls, there are plenty of advantages. You'll save money on clothes, they'll have twice as many toys to play with, bedroom-sharing either at home or on holiday will be acceptable well into their teens, and with any luck they will grow up to be best friends with lots of shared interests.

TODDLER 🄰🄱🄲

Breaking the News

When to tell your toddler about the baby really depends on when you want other people to know. This is because he's bound to blurt it out once he knows. And he'll overhear you telling others about the baby so it's important that you've actually told him yourself – even non-speaking 1-year-olds will understand a little of what you're chatting about to other people.

In a quiet moment, when he's in a good mood, tell him that there's a baby in your tummy and that one day it will come out and he can play with it. You can follow this chat with children's books about mum having a baby.

Even if the age gap between your children is very close and your eldest is pre-verbal – still take the time to explain to him about the baby. From 6 months he'll be old enough to share books about new babies (a few minutes pointing to the pictures) and by a year you can read the books to him. If they're simple your toddler will probably understand quite a lot of what's going on despite not being able to talk yet.

As your pregnancy progresses you can show your toddler your tummy if he's interested, and perhaps even feel the baby kicking in the latter months.

Young children have little concept of time and may expect the baby to appear hours after you break the news. So explain that there's a long wait ahead – perhaps find something seasonal to make comparisons with, for example the baby will come when the apples on the tree are big enough to eat, or when the trees have green leaves on them again.

Teaching Independence

Teaching your toddler to do things for himself will make things much easier once the baby arrives. The sooner you start, the better, because trying to rush this in the last few weeks will be ineffective. This is because toddlers often regress at around the time of the birth, behaving in a more babyish way than usual, so they certainly won't want to learn new skills.

But in the meantime you can go ahead and teach your toddler a few skills. It's realistic to expect some toddlers to feed themselves with a spoon from about a year old (it takes about 3 months to become proficient), and to be able to get undressed as they approach the age of 2. Most children begin by pulling off T-shirts and elasticated trousers or skirts, but will still struggle for a few more months with jumpers and tights. Learning to get dressed takes a little longer – from about 2½ you can expect your child to be able to put on some items of clothing, including his shoes. It takes until at least 3½ before a child can reliably put his shoes on the right feet.

Do note that pyjamas are relatively easy to put on – from 20 months you can put the top over your child's head, then ask him to put his own arms in.

And if you give him plenty of praise and encouragement he should soon start to learn to put the bottoms on, too – just remind him to sit down or he'll fall over.

Children vary greatly in how compliant and willing they are to learn. If your toddler is particularly boisterous and energetic, you may have to add at least 6 months to each of these milestones.

TIME SAVER

A simple task that all children over 18 months can start to learn is to take their shoes off when you get home and leave them in a particular place in the hall – this means you won't waste time searching for them next time you go out. Of everything you teach your child, this is one of the most time-saving tasks he can learn, so it's worth putting the effort in now.

Getting Him into a 'Big Bed'

Your toddler can go into a big bed from the age of about 2, but if he is very agile or tall he may need to be out of his cot by around 18 months – once he is 91cm (3ft) he will be tall enough to climb out quite easily. If you think he'll be out of his cot before or soon after the arrival of your new baby, aim to get him used to his new big bed well in advance.

Your toddler is bound to get out of bed once he realizes that he is no longer contained in his cot and it will probably take a couple of weeks of patient persistence as you calmly take him back to bed before he co-operates. So if you can get this rather tedious process out of the way before the baby arrives, it will be a big advantage.

Routine

When it comes to coping with a baby and toddler, we highly recommend a routine. You may well have your toddler in a routine already, and you can work on tightening this up between now and the birth of your baby.

If you've got some sort of structure and pattern to your day, you'll find it easier to fit your baby into your toddler's day-to-day life. And what's more, there will be less change for your toddler when the baby arrives.

It's one thing to go with the flow when you've got just one child, but with two very young children you'll need to run things more like a military operation, particularly in the first year.

If a routine doesn't appeal, rest assured that as your children get older you'll be able to have a more relaxed timetable. In the meantime, a typical routine for a 2-year-old would be to wake at about 7 a.m., breakfast at 7.30ish, lunch at 11.30/12, a 2-hour afternoon nap, dinner at about 5 p.m., a bath at 6 p.m. and into bed by 7 p.m. Of course you can move this forward or even back by an hour, and juggle mealtimes a bit. The key is to stick to a similar pattern each day.

Having a routine in place will mean that your toddler will feel tired or hungry at around the same time each day, enabling you to plan ahead and respond quickly to his needs – this will hopefully avoid too many meltdowns.

We particularly recommend getting a bedtime routine in place, if you haven't done so already. On a particularly fractious day it can be a huge comfort to be able to look at the clock and know that your toddler will be sound asleep in, say, 2 hours' time. We know from experience that this can be a sanity-saver when you're coping with a new baby and a toddler.

With your toddler's bedtime routine, there are two things that will help when the baby arrives. First, sticking to an agreed number of stories each night (one or two) and not being pushed beyond this – it's very easy to get into negotiations and arguments about the number of stories if the rules haven't been set in stone. And secondly, encourage your toddler to play by himself for 10 minutes after his bath (longer if possible) while you get on with other things such as sorting laundry and, in a few months' time, dressing or feeding your baby. If your toddler is in the habit of playing by himself each night, this will make life considerably easier after the birth of your baby.

Getting into a routine obviously takes time and effort, but the payback will be immense because your toddler will be in the right mindset for what's coming next and be more likely to co-operate.

So, as well as bedtime, try to get your toddler into the habit of regular mealtimes, sitting at the table or in a high chair. Encourage your child to sit still for 3 meals a day, as this will be a huge help when the baby arrives. Take time to sit and eat with him and resist rushing about – having your attention during mealtimes will help your toddler to enjoy them more. You can always save your rushing about for dessert – if he's eating ice-cream he's unlikely to notice if you start clearing up. You can also try getting your child to sit at the table for snacks, because this will not only help teach table manners, but making snacks part of the routine means no grazing. Grazing can make mealtimes tricky, as your toddler won't be hungry.

It's also worth getting routines in place for getting up and leaving the house. Your toddler will know what to expect, and in the morning you'll be able to operate on auto-pilot, which will make you less likely to forget things such as wipes and topping-up water bottles. The more tired you are, the more you forget – which is when a routine really comes into its own.

Of course there will be days when your toddler refuses to co-operate, or when appointments or social plans throw the routine out of kilter. When this happens, just let it go and start again the next day. It's very important not to become so routine-obsessed that being out of your routine actually becomes a source of stress. The purpose of having a structure and pattern to your day is to *reduce* your stress, not increase it. So never aim for perfection. After all, in the workplace if a meeting overruns by 40 minutes no one really notices, let alone gets their knickers in a twist about it. And toddlers can't tell the time.

Arrange Childcare

Get childcare in place so that your toddler doesn't feel suddenly rejected when the baby arrives. Ideally this should be sorted out at least a couple of months before the birth – the longer, the better. It may seem extravagant paying for extra childcare before your baby is actually born, but the cost is worth it because your child will feel so much more settled. And of course it will give you a chance to put your feet up – or, more likely, rush around and get things done.

If Grandma is going to be helping out, encourage her to come and help before the baby is born so that your older child becomes used to spending time with her alone if you're not around.

CHILD

When it comes to telling your child about the baby, you can make him feel important by breaking the news to him before you tell other people. Explain that he'll be even more important in the baby's life than Grandma and Grandpa, which is why you're telling him first. Then when he hears you telling other people, he'll feel special. You could even let him be the one to make the announcement to grandparents and close family members. Be prepared for your child to tell all sorts of people, including those at school or nursery.

As with toddlers, books about new babies can be helpful. Answer any questions he may have about how the baby got there as simply and honestly as you can. If your child isn't interested in talking about the baby, then avoid the subject.

You'll also need to decide whether to wait until you are 12 weeks pregnant before telling your child, when your risk of miscarriage is reduced. In many ways this makes sense because you won't have to explain a miscarriage to your child should the worst happen (and also have to explain to anyone he may have told).

But children are resilient and most would cope with a simple and truthful explanation – and this is certainly better than your child seeing you very upset and not understanding why. The best decision depends on numerous factors – here are some to consider:

- Are you someone who keeps emotions and feelings quietly to yourself?
- Do you suffer badly from morning sickness?
- Did it take a long time to conceive this baby? If so, it may feel as though you are tempting fate by telling your child too soon.
- Is your child observant and sensitive?
- Is your child easy-going and unlikely to notice that anything is different?

There's no right or wrong time to tell your child – it's an individual decision which you alone are the best person to make.

Do note that older toddlers and children may feel afraid of what might happen when the baby arrives. So when you reach about 7 months in your pregnancy, your child's behaviour may become atrocious and you may start getting complaints from school or nursery. Try to be patient – your child is probably feeling upset, scared, worried and generally overwhelmed. The good news is that things often calm down once the baby arrives and your child discovers that the reality isn't so bad.

HOUSEKEEPING

You'll have plenty of baby paraphernalia already, but you'll still have to go out and buy some things. Here's a list of the things you may need.

A double buggy – if your toddler will be under 2½ when the baby is born, this is worth investing in. The large-wheeled models where one child sits in front of the other (tandem style) work best in our experience: your toddler won't be able to reach the baby and these are easier to manoeuvre than the wide, side-by-side models that tend to be harder to push and tricky to get into doorways. One downside is that the view from the back seat of the buggy isn't as good as from the front seat. But on balance we think this is still the best option, as you'll be out and about so much more often.

A buggy board – these can work if your toddler will be between 2½ and 4 when the baby is born. Most children need either a ride on the buggy board or in a buggy from time to time until they are about 4. The downside of buggy boards is that they can make pushing a buggy uncomfortable, and mounting obstacles or curbs more difficult, so you may want to borrow and try out a buggy board before you buy one. If you don't like it you may think it is worth buying a double buggy – or possibly looking for a single-seater buggy that also has a built-in platform for a toddler or an older child to stand on.

A baby sling – this is invaluable when you have your second baby (see Chapter 5 for more on this). We recommend an Ergo baby carrier, as lots of parents say this is the most comfortable.

A second cot – if your toddler will be under 2 when your baby is born, you'll need a second cot. Your new baby can be in a Moses basket until the age of about 2 months, after which she'll need to go in a proper cot. And your toddler will need to be in a cot until about the age of 2.

Mattresses – you'll have to buy new mattresses for the Moses basket and cot to reduce the risk of cot death – every baby needs her own new mattress.

Nappy kit – you'll need to buy newborn nappies, cotton wool, nappy bags and a changing mat. If you went for washable nappies with your first baby, you'll probably want to do the same with your second. But do bear in mind that lots of parents end up putting their second baby in disposable nappies despite initial good intentions – coping with extra laundry and nappy leaks isn't easy when you've got two children. Opting for biodegradable nappies, which decompose more quickly in landfill sites, is a good compromise.

Feeding kit – if you intend to breastfeed, then stock up on breast pads, batteries for your breast pump (if you used one) and nipple cream if you suffered from sore nipples – unfortunately this problem often recurs with subsequent babies. You may also need to buy more maternity bras, as lots of women are bigger with subsequent babies.

If you intend to bottle-feed, ensure you have newborn formula, bottles with slow-flow teats, and that your sterilizer still works.

TROUBLESHOOTING

My older child still wakes at night – how do I get him sleeping through?

Toddlers and young children wake at night from time to time for any number of reasons such as teething, bed-wetting, nightmares and so on. If it's not more than about once a week there's no point in trying to change anything, because your child will gradually wake up less as he gets older. However, if your child wakes frequently for a bit of comfort in the night, you need to break the habit. You can teach your child to soothe himself to sleep rather than depend on you, so begin by focusing on bedtime. If he can soothe himself at bedtime, he'll be able to do it in the night, too – we all wake up several times a night but mostly go straight back to sleep not even remembering that we awoke. So aim at bedtime to be able to kiss your child goodnight, then leave the room. Don't lie next to him while he falls asleep, or even stay in the room – your aim is to teach him to fall asleep alone. This can take over a week and your child may become pretty angry, but persist and you'll soon get results. Explain that once you've kissed him goodnight there's no more talking, then if he gets out of bed lead him gently but silently back to bed, being sure not to engage in conversation. Give him another kiss, then leave.

My toddler refuses most foods at mealtimes, then demands constant snacks

You can banish any fussy eating problems by presenting your child with 3 meals a day and then being indifferent as to whether or not he eats. You'll see results within about 4 days. This sounds very simple, but you have to be prepared for him to eat nothing at some meals and you'll need a lot of willpower not to give in and offer him alternative meals or snacks when he gets hungry. You can give him a pre-planned snack such as a banana or yoghurt between meals, but stick to this. Also don't be tempted to let him fill up on milk – a pint (550ml) a day (including milk used on cereal, etc.) is plenty for toddlers aged over 1.

If you happen to be suffering from morning sickness, this can actually be an advantage because feeling too sick to coax and cajole, let alone cook something else, will make the process easier. Your child will soon realize that refusing food no longer gets him any attention – instead mum seems in quite a hurry to clear up the meal and get on and do something else. As long as your toddler is having enough to drink, he won't come to any harm. So don't feel guilty if he only seems to eat a few mouthfuls of food a day and becomes irritable between meals. In the long term you're doing him a huge favour.

My older child still breastfeeds

When you are about 5 months into your pregnancy, your milk will change to colostrum and there will be less of it. When this happens, lots of older babies don't like the taste and decide for themselves to stop breastfeeding – so nature takes care of the situation. But if your baby wants to continue feeding, there's no reason why he shouldn't and you can even tandem-feed once your baby is born – feeding two babies at once. If this isn't for you, then be sure to wean your older baby well before the birth of your second to ensure that he doesn't feel rejected.

My child is old enough to start potty-training, should I try?

It's very tempting to get your eldest out of nappies before your baby is born, and this will certainly make life a bit easier. But what will make life harder is if he isn't really ready and you end up having to clear up lots of accidents and the whole process becomes stressful. What you can do is try for a couple of days, then assess whether your child is ready or if he would be better waiting until a few months after the baby is born. So buy a potty and some pants and, if your toddler seems interested, put him in pants for a morning and see if he manages to use the potty. Try this for a couple of days and you'll soon see whether he hasn't got a clue and randomly wees on the floor, or if he actively tries to use the potty – perhaps managing a couple of times, or at least attempting to get to the potty on time – in which case he's probably ready to learn. As a general guide, girls tend to be ready at about 2¼ and boys at 2½ – but this is a very rough estimate and plenty of children start much later. Make sure that potty-training is child-led, so if your toddler isn't keen, pack the potty and pants away until at least 3 months after your baby is born. And don't be tempted to try for the first time in the last 2 months before your due date.

I've heard that I'm not supposed to lift now that I'm pregnant, but I've got a toddler and this advice isn't practical

Pregnancy hormones make your ligaments looser and your joints more supple, which means that you are more likely to pull something, especially if you lift. But if you are careful, keep yourself symmetrical and bend your knees, lifting your toddler should be OK. The most important thing is to listen to your body and stop if you get just the tiniest hint that lifting is a bad idea. It's worth taking time to teach your toddler to climb up and down the stairs by himself, because carrying a toddler upstairs is particularly hard on your body, especially as you get bigger. As your belly grows, your centre of gravity alters, making it even more likely that you will injure yourself. So try to taper off how often you lift your toddler, even if everything takes twice as long. If you have plenty of cuddles sitting down he shouldn't notice too much, but there will be the occasion when he's refusing to move and you need to pick him up. When this happens, do remember to bend your knees and not twist awkwardly, and take your time, however stressful the situation seems.

CHAPTER 2

The Final Weeks and Days Before the Birth

Suddenly the birth of your new baby is imminent and you're probably dashing about trying to get organized. If your to-do list seems insurmountable, don't panic – you'll be surprised at how easy you'll find looking after a newborn baby compared with first time around, and it will still be possible to get things done once your baby is born. So split your list up – things that you absolutely have to do before the birth, and things that can wait.

You'll almost certainly feel even more tired than you did at the end of your last pregnancy, and your midwife is no doubt telling you to get plenty of rest. In an ideal world you'd be having afternoon naps and early nights. But if this isn't happening, we suggest that you slump in front of the television with your toddler, as this counts as rest – so do this whenever you can. Some women feel extremely tired just before going into labour – if this happens to you, then do whatever you can to cancel everything so that you can sleep. Listening to your body and getting some rest will certainly help when it comes to giving birth.

MUM

You probably had your hospital bag, notes and birth plan packed weeks before the birth of your first child. But with the second this can sometimes get left until very late. Do make time to do this, as you'll instantly feel less stressed.

If you're having a home birth, then ensure that you have plastic sheets to protect your home. You may also want lots of pillows – you can place these in plastic bags, then pillow cases, and you'll need strong bin liners for both laundry and waste after the birth. If you're planning a water birth, ensure that your partner knows how to assemble the pool – practise building if possible.

Bending becomes increasingly difficult as you get towards the end of your pregnancy. Second time around it will be particularly challenging as you may be bigger, and also having a small child requires you to bend down more often. With a bit of planning you can reduce how often you need to bend – for example, if your toddler is still in nappies and you change him on the floor, set up a changing table so that you can stand up for nappy changes. When it comes to getting your toddler dressed, sit on the bed with him on your knee. This is more comfortable than bending over him to put on, for example, his trousers, which can also put strain on your back. Similarly for shoes, you can sit on the stairs to help him. Or you can sit your toddler in his high chair – he can't run away and you can position yourself more comfortably than squatting over him on the floor. Getting down on all fours works well for picking up toys, and getting into this position for 10 minutes twice a day is thought to relieve pregnancy-related back pain and may even help get the baby into a better position for birth.

Birth

Second deliveries tend to be quicker and more straightforward. This is because the uterus, having laboured once, functions more efficiently the second time around, and the long latent phase of labour from a closed cervix to established labour (3-cm dilation) is much shorter second time around as the cervix 'ripens' much more easily because it has opened before. Coupled with the fact that your perineum and vagina stretch more easily if you've given birth before, you're less likely to need intervention such as forceps, ventouse or an episiotomy.

And with second babies, your risk of pre-eclampsia (high blood pressure in late pregnancy that can lead to an emergency Caesarean) and a post-partum haemorrhage (bleeding straight after the baby is born) are reduced.

You'll hopefully be less afraid second time around and so produce fewer stress hormones, which are thought to slow labour. The pain will seem less alarming and you'll have more of a resigned 'here we go again' attitude rather than feeling bewildered and anxious about the unknown. Even the midwives are more relaxed with women who have given birth before, and the low-key atmosphere will further help to keep you calm, making your labour swifter and so reducing your chance of needing an epidural. This obviously does not apply if your first delivery was by Caesarean (see Chapter 1).

Speedy Labour – How to Slow Things Down

If your last labour was quick, chances are your next labour will be speedy, too, perhaps even faster than last time. Keep your notes and hospital telephone number with you at all times, and call the hospital the moment you go into labour so that they can be ready. To slow things down you can lie on your left side – but call your midwife if you're having a home birth, or get to hospital as quickly as you can.

BABY

Your first baby's head may have moved down into your pelvis at around 36 weeks, but this time your baby's head may not engage until you are in labour.

Your second baby may not make such a clear announcement that she's coming as your first baby did. This is because Braxton Hicks contractions can be stronger and more painful with each baby that you have, and this can be mistaken for labour. So you are more likely to have a false alarm when you think the baby is coming, then not actually go into labour for another week. A downside of this is childcare – Grandma or your sister comes charging over, only to be sent home again.

Warn them in advance that this may happen, then don't be afraid to call when you go into 'labour' again. What you don't want is to be in labour but not have any childcare because you weren't sure if it was the real thing – this is very stressful as you'll end up taking your toddler with you to hospital, and labour could well be quick. Here are some differences between a false labour and the real thing:

Braxton Hicks Contractions

- Won't open your cervix
- Give you pain all over your tummy
- Vary in length
- Don't become stronger, longer and closer
- May stop or slow down if you move around or rest

Real Contractions

- Will open your cervix
- Cause pain lower down
- Last 30 seconds or longer and are fairly regular
- Will become stronger, longer and closer as a sustained rhythm becomes apparent
- Won't be affected if you move around or rest

Remember that if your waters break you'll need to call your childcare whether or not you are getting contractions, because the midwife will want to deliver your baby within 24 hours to avoid the risk of infection. Call the hospital when you start to get contractions – an experienced midwife will keep you on the phone for about 10 minutes and be able to tell if you are in labour and how far along you are.

If you start getting contractions before week 37, you'll need to get to hospital immediately because smaller, premature babies come more quickly – and, coupled with the fact that this is your second baby, you will have even less time.

TODDLER 🅐🅑🅒

It's too late to 'train' your toddler in the final weeks before the birth, so don't embark on any dramatic new sleep or eating regimes. You can of course iron out any problems you've been working on, but be very gentle because children are good at picking up on stress and your toddler will no doubt be sensing the imminent arrival of his sibling. Use the last few days to spend time sitting quietly with your child, cuddling, chatting and reading stories. Perhaps you can find a really special story that you can continue to read to your toddler after the baby is born – young children love repetition and find it comforting, especially when so much will have changed with the arrival of the baby.

If your bump becomes so big that your toddler can no longer sit comfortably on your knee, do 'share' in how annoying it is that the baby has grown so much that you can't even sit comfortably together for a story – keep it light and if possible joke about it. And try sitting your toddler next to you with a blanket over your knees so that he still feels connected and cozy. Hopefully this will help your toddler not to feel too rejected before the baby is even born.

You can keep the blanket for after the baby is born, then use it in the same way to encourage your toddler to sit next to you while you feed the baby. Ensure you never use this particular blanket for the baby, and refer to it as 'our' snuggle blanket (yours and your toddler's). This gives your toddler a clear message that you value the bond between you and him, even when you are feeding the baby. This won't of course work for all toddlers, and certainly not every day, but we have plenty more ideas for breastfeeding with a toddler in the coming chapters.

You can ask your toddler the sex of the baby if you haven't found out already – it's uncanny how small children often get this right (although admittedly they do have a one-in-two chance of being right, and scans are obviously far more reliable …).

If he's interested, show your toddler where the new baby will sleep, bath, have her nappies changed and keep her clothes. Talk about how he can help look after his new sibling. And do refer to it as your child's new baby brother or sister to help him feel involved – this also helps to keep him feeling centre stage. You can also talk about 'our baby'. Try to avoid saying 'my baby'.

Explain that the baby will be a bit boring at first and won't even be able to smile. Tell your toddler that the baby won't be able to walk or talk but will cry a lot by saying 'waaa' – but this is nothing to worry about, all babies cry because it's their way of 'talking' and asking for milk.

Talk to your toddler about labour – even if you're not having a home birth, the chances are he'll see you in the early stages of labour. Explain that when the baby is big enough to come out, she'll let you know by making your tummy hurt. Act out what's going to happen – rubbing your abdomen, breathing noisily, groaning, going on all fours – if possible make your child laugh. Perhaps say, 'Ow, OK, baby, we know you're ready and want to come out,' which will demonstrate that the pain is nothing to be alarmed about. In our experience, children are remarkably unfazed about Mum being in labour.

Tell your child the next stage of your plan, for example 'Daddy will drive Mummy to the hospital.' And take time to explain who will look after your toddler while you're away.

Explain to your child that once the baby is born you'll be tired and will need to sleep sometimes during the day. But that the baby will give him a present. It can be easier for small children to look forward to a present than a new baby – and this time-tested strategy of buying a gift for the older child certainly helps get the sibling relationship off to a positive start.

CHILD

Only talk to your child about the baby if he's interested – if he asks questions, then this is the ideal time to talk. You can try telling him about what life will be like when the baby is born, and tell him what will change and what won't. For example, Dad will do the school or nursery run instead of Mum, he'll still go to football club on Saturdays, but you won't be able to go swimming with him after school on Fridays until the baby is old enough to come, too – although he can have pizza and a DVD as his Friday after-school treat instead.

Most children, and toddlers too, ask questions about how the baby got there and how it will get out. Our advice is to answer as simply and as honestly as possible. It's actually a very natural and appropriate way for young children to start to understand about reproduction and sex.

Older children may also worry about your safety and could well have overheard anxious conversations you may have had about giving birth. So do give your child reassurance about both the labour and delivery – perhaps talk about what happened when he was born, but obviously keep any horror stories to yourself.

HOUSEKEEPING

Preparing Your Home

Aim to make your home bomb-proof so that your toddler can run riot when you are looking after your baby. You've probably done this to a certain extent already, but just tighten things up a bit. Between the ages of 14 and 24 months, your toddler is likely to empty cupboards and drawers (ensure knives and anything dangerous are out of reach), and from 16 months he'll be fiddling with knobs on the cooker and washing machine (think about how to keep him out of the kitchen). You may also want to move computers to rooms that you can keep shut, and even store away ornaments and floor lamps for a few months, as this will give you less to watch out for. Ensure medicines are locked away – and this includes iron supplements, which can kill a toddler if too many are eaten.

A stair gate at the top of the stairs can work well for bathtime as it enables you to keep your toddler contained upstairs while you bath the baby. And a lock on the outside of your bedroom door (placed high up) will prevent your toddler from disturbing the baby during nap times. If you haven't already done so, check that all cord-operated window blinds have safety mechanisms on them – buy and install these if necessary (they're relatively cheap and easily fitted). Toddlers and young children have been known to become caught up on loose window blind cords or chains, causing strangulation.

Ask for Help

Now is the ideal time to ask for help with all the extra jobs that will need doing. After your baby has arrived it will probably sound like criticism to suddenly ask your partner or even your mother-in-law to, for example, put the washing on – especially as you'll be tired and more likely to snap. It's much better to say, 'Let me show you how the washing machine works; I won't get a chance once the baby is here.' Likewise, you can say this to any other 'helpers' you may have lined up, such as a friend, a cleaner or a home help.

Childcare Arrangements

While you're in hospital giving birth, you'll obviously need someone to look after your other child (this applies even if you're having a home birth so that you're not having to worry).

The most straightforward arrangement is to persuade a relative, such as Grandma, to stay at your home for a couple of nights – this is the least disruptive for your toddler. Of course you'll talk about the plans, but it's helpful to write down your toddler's routine as well as details of where to find his food in the freezer and so on.

However, if Grandma, or whoever has agreed, happens to live a long way away, you'll need to arrange for a neighbour or someone local who is willing to look after your toddler for a couple of hours should your labour progress very quickly and you have to dash to hospital. Make sure they are prepared to come at 4 a.m. We suggest having a couple of back-ups in case people are ill or there is some other valid last-minute reason why they can't help.

An alternative is to arrange for your toddler to stay with relatives or friends – you'll need to have an overnight bag packed for your child, and decide how he's getting to them – is he being picked up or are you dropping him off? Do talk to him about this, as it may be a bit stressful for your toddler, especially if it ends up happening in the middle of the night. But if you've explained in advance what is happening, your toddler will cope – even if he cries when you leave him. It's normal for children under the age of about 5 to sometimes become tearful when being left by Mum, and this will be exacerbated by the fact that your toddler will pick up on the stress of you being in labour and rushing to hospital.

Arranging Help for After the Birth

Lots of mums muddle through on their own without help, and in this book this is what we are assuming you will do. But it's going to be a busy time, so if you are lucky enough to have some help that's very good news. If you've got a willing relative, or indeed the money to pay for some help, then try to anticipate what will be most useful to you. Perhaps you detest endless laundry and cleaning up sticky meals – if this is the case, then a cleaner could be a good option. Or maybe you hate broken nights and a lack of sleep – think about a maternity nurse or someone to take both children for a couple of hours every morning while you catch up on sleep. If you're dreading tea and bathtime, you could get some help from around 5 p.m. Plan what you think will be most useful – you can always change your mind once your baby is born.

Filling the Freezer and Stocking Your Larder

Aim to get at least a week's worth of frozen meals for your toddler or child, plus some meals for you and your partner that you can freeze. Ideally choose food that you can all share, such as casseroles and shepherd's pie. But if you're short of time, get your child's meals organized and buy some frozen ready meals for yourself and your partner – you can also dig out some takeaway menus.

If you stock up on the following you'll be able to postpone your first post-baby shopping trip by a couple of days:

- For the freezer: oven chips, vegetables, berries, bread
- For the larder: eggs, baked beans, tins of minestrone soup, long-life milk

This will enable to you eat egg and chips, beans on toast, smoothies (long life milk and frozen berries), and minestrone (a complete meal). And stock up on essentials such as toilet paper, cleaning products and breakfast cereal – buy as much as you've got storage space for.

You can also buy plenty of tea and biscuits or wine and crisps for visitors. By offering a snack you'll make it clear, should you want to, that you're not going to be cooking them a meal even if they happen to turn up at lunchtime.

Gift from the Baby

Buy a present for your baby to 'give' to your older child. Choose something you know your child will really love, ideally something you've resisted buying up until now such as a Barbie doll, Power Ranger figure or Lego set. Because although such toys may be a little 'old' for your child at the moment, they will guarantee a 'wow' reaction. Aim for indulgence and nothing too sensible. And avoid toys that have 'expectation' – a colouring book expects your toddler to sit quietly, a baby doll expects him to be interested in babies. Such toys will be useful in later weeks, but not as presents from the new baby. Pack the gift in your hospital bag in case your toddler visits the baby in hospital – of course you may well be home so quickly that this doesn't happen, in which case you can give it to him at home.

Do Some Grocery Shopping Online

Once you've bought your groceries a couple of times online, your 'favourites' will automatically pop up when you sign onto the site. This is very useful for when your baby has arrived and you find yourself with 'baby-brain' and need a bit of help remembering what to buy.

Visit the Discount Shop

Stock up on cheap toys to occupy your older child once the baby arrives. You can also start collecting arts and crafts materials – cereal boxes, old greetings cards, old magazines (children particularly like baby magazines), glue, sticky tape, coloured pencils, paper, notebooks and so on.

Find Vases

You may be sent flowers, even for a second baby.

TROUBLESHOOTING

My toddler isn't in a routine, and I feel very unprepared and disorganized

Of course it helps if your oldest is in some sort of routine and able to do things for himself. But this often doesn't happen, especially if you've got a particularly boisterous child or a close age gap. But life doesn't stop once you have a new baby, or at least not for more than a few weeks. You'll soon find that you have enough time to focus on your older child and nudge him into better eating and sleeping habits.

My child has been in trouble at school recently and I'm sure it's because he's worried about the baby, but when I talk to him he's not interested

It's normal for children to feel anxious before the birth of a sibling, and play up. Explain to your child, briefly but clearly, who will look after him when you go into labour. Once you've done this, only mention the baby if he does. Although it's tempting to have a reassuring chat with your child, this is unlikely to be helpful – children generally respond better to having a really good play session with a parent and find this far more comforting. It doesn't have to be for long – 15 minutes is OK – but you do have to give your child your undivided attention, so avoid your mobile and computer and just focus on him. Story books about new babies and siblings can be useful – but again, don't force these on your child. Let him decide if he wants you to read these to him, or he might have a peep at them when you're not looking.

When I was pregnant with my eldest, I felt I almost knew him before he was born – this hasn't happened this time

With a first pregnancy it's normal to spend hours reading up on fetal development so that you know the exact size and advancement of your baby each week. You probably gazed at your scan pictures for hours, and perhaps even had a nickname for your unborn baby. It's no wonder you felt connected. This time you will have been far too busy focusing on your other child, but this won't affect the bonding process in any way once your new baby is born. And the advantage of having a busy pregnancy is that you won't have had as much time to worry about things going wrong. We're all haunted by scary 'What if?' scenarios when we're pregnant and it's no bad thing if we haven't got time for too many of these.

CHAPTER 3
Bringing Your Baby Home

When you suddenly have a new baby in your home it is very exciting, particularly for your eldest. Perhaps you'll arrive home from hospital to a stampede of little feet as your child rushes to greet you, or if you had a home birth your eldest may wake to discover his sibling has arrived during the night.

Unlike with your first baby, you won't feel daunted and overwhelmed by the task of looking after a newborn. You'll be able to change nappies with lightning efficiency, feeding and winding will be second nature, and you'll pop on sleepsuits without accidentally twisting your baby's arms. Even if you've had a longer age gap, you'll find your baby-skills come back very quickly.

Your new challenge this time will be managing your eldest's reaction to his sibling. In most cases this will go well, as children are usually delighted to have a brand new baby brother or sister. But sometimes children are unimpressed by their new sibling and, indeed, angry and jealous from the first meeting. There's plenty you can do to smooth the first meeting and handle adverse responses.

MUM

Depending on your birth, you'll either be out of hospital within 24 hours of having your baby, or if you had complications or a Caesarean you'll be kept in for a few days. If you get any choice in the matter, consider staying in hospital for a little longer. Even though this will mean being away from your firstborn for another night, it's better to have a little more time to recover than to arrive home still in the after-shock of labour.

Likewise if you've had a home birth, stay in bed for at least a day. As soon as you get up and dressed, everyone will assume you're fully recovered and you'll find yourself back in your role of running the household. Let others do this for as long as possible – however haphazardly.

Giving birth to second and subsequent babies is usually easier and less traumatic than first time around. But if this wasn't the case, do take time to talk it through with a doctor or a midwife. If you can understand exactly why, for example, you ended up with an emergency Caesarean, you'll find it easier to accept.

As your womb contracts, it can be extremely painful – far worse than with your first baby. After-pain can last for a few days and you'll probably need painkillers. Paracetamol and codeine (which is stronger) are both safe to take while breastfeeding. Do note that codeine can cause constipation after a couple of days, and if taken for more than 3 weeks, can be addictive for some people.

You may find it quite emotional suddenly having two (or more) children, and your feelings will probably be quite up and down. Perhaps you feel very protective towards your tiny fragile new baby, and your toddler suddenly looks like a great thumping baboon with attitude. Or maybe your newborn's demands seem overwhelming and tedious and you feel much closer to your amusing, delightful firstborn. And you may simply feel overwhelmed by the amount of love you feel for both your children. Whatever you're feeling it will probably be quite extreme – your hormones are crazy and you've just given birth. But give yourself time for everything to settle and try not to let 'worry' be added to your already complicated emotions. And if you don't feel overwhelmed with love for either your baby or your older child at the moment, this will change – probably within the next few days.

Breastfeeding

If you breastfed last time you'll be a pro, but your baby will be new to breastfeeding and will take a little time to learn. So be patient and give her plenty of help latching on. You'll notice that feeding your baby may seem a little different to feeding your first-born – intriguingly, all babies feed slightly differently – some are efficient, some are sleepy, others get confused.

If you didn't breastfeed last time, don't let this put you off having another go. But ask for help, because the midwives will probably assume you know what you're doing as this is your second baby. Some babies seem naturally quicker at learning to breastfeed than others, so perhaps you'll be luckier with your baby this time and find it easier – also you'll be more relaxed with your second baby than your first. But however difficult breastfeeding seems at first, remember that it is possible to learn this skill. You just need a good teacher (keep pestering the midwives for help) and perseverance. In an ideal world you'd breastfeed your baby for at least 6 months, but even if you just manage a few feeds, your baby will benefit. This is because the yellow colostrum milk, produced in the first few days before your milk 'comes in', is packed with antibodies and protective white cells to boost your baby's immunity and help ward off bacteria and viruses. It takes about 2 weeks for colostrum to be completely replaced by the thinner, whiter milk. Of course the benefits of breastfeeding continue over the months, and the longer you feed the better. And although initially it will be more challenging to breastfeed when you've got an older child than it would be to bottle-feed, by about month 3 when your baby is feeding more regularly, breastfeeding will seem more convenient. But if you don't think breastfeeding will work for you in the long term, you could consider giving your baby some colostrum-rich feeds in the first couple of weeks when you've hopefully got people around to help out with your older child.

BABY

Like all new babies, this one will no doubt feed non-stop, especially at night, and will probably sleep a lot during the day. Being asleep during the day can be frustrating for your older child, so when the baby does wake up, be sure to call him over. Newborns can't stay awake for more than about 90 minutes and your baby will need feeding and a nappy change during this time, which doesn't leave much play time for your eldest.

At this age your baby may recognize her sibling's voice from when she was in the womb, but she won't be able to focus on him, let alone interact. But you can show your eldest how to touch your baby's palm so that she'll grip it, and also touch the sole of her foot so that she curls her toes. Babies are born with these primitive reflexes. Enjoy them while they last because your baby will grow out of these after a couple of months.

Second babies are more likely to catch a cold in the early days than first-borns because they catch them from their siblings. You can take preventative measures by wiping or washing your eldest's hands before he touches the baby – wash everyone's hands so that he doesn't feel like the germ-ridden pariah. This is actually a clever way of getting visitors to wash their hands without seeming like a fusspot.

If your baby does catch a cold in the early days there are some simple steps you can take. Put a folded towel under her mattress beneath her head to prop her up slightly and help clear her nasal passages – this will help the mucus drain into her stomach. Use saline nose drops (from chemists) to clear her nasal passages – your baby won't like these, but if she's struggling to feed because her nose is blocked they are very useful. And, if you're feeling brave, suck the mucus from your infant's nose, then spit it out. This isn't as disgusting as it sounds and is an effective way of clearing your baby's nasal passages – plenty of mums resort to this.

What you're trying to avoid is dehydration, which can occur when your baby swallows a lot of mucus so vomits up a milk feed, or struggles to feed in the first place because her nose is blocked. She should have around 8 wet nappies a day in the first 2 weeks – if she has fewer than 4, you should be concerned.

TIPS FOR ESTABLISHING A ROUTINE

Don't worry about trying to keep your eldest quiet so that the baby can sleep – it's inevitable that she's going to grow up in a noisy household, and the sooner she gets used to it, the better. A bit of gentle prodding and noise from an exuberant toddler will help your baby get her body clock sorted out as she learns the difference between night and day.

TODDLER ABC

Whether your toddler meets his sibling during a visit to the hospital or when you bring the baby home, be sure to greet your child like a long-lost friend and make a huge fuss of him – after all, he's just had what was probably his first night away from you. So make sure you're not holding the baby when you first see your toddler, then you can give him a big hug.

Only then mention the baby and ask if he'd like to meet her. Your toddler will probably want to touch the baby, so let him tickle her toes – this keeps his hands well away from her eyes and hopefully won't wake her if she's asleep (babies aren't ticklish until they are 6 months old). He can also stroke the baby's tummy and try prompting the baby's primitive reflexes as mentioned on page 34.

Compliment your toddler on how gentle he's being, and resist telling him off if he's rough – he's extremely unlikely to do any harm as your new baby will be much tougher than she looks. She's just been squeezed through your birth canal or yanked out by Caesarean, both of which are far more vigorous than an over-zealous toddler hug (or even a thump!). If he's accidently a bit rough it will upset and confuse him to be told off, and if he's trying it on a bit he'll get rewarded with attention, even if it's negative attention. Instead, tell him in a neutral voice, 'We don't hurt the baby,' then play a game of how lightly you can touch each other's hands. This will distract him from the baby, give him the one-to-one attention he obviously craves, and also teach him to touch gently.

One of the delights of having his own sibling is that he'll have far more access to the new baby compared with other babies he may have encountered. He'll love being allowed to tickle, prod and stroke his new sibling, so give him as much freedom (supervised, of course) as you dare.

With any luck, when your children meet for the first time it will be very sweet and quite wonderful. However, there are plenty of alternatives to the rather idyllic scene we all hope for. So don't be surprised if your toddler becomes bored after a few minutes and wants to do something else – toddlers have very short attention spans. Now would be a good time to give him the present from the baby.

Sometimes toddlers don't even want to look at the new baby. This is fairly standard and nothing to worry about – it sometimes happens if there was a lot of build-up and expectation before the baby arrived. Resist the temptation to force this relationship; simply give your toddler lots of attention and let him become curious in his own time.

How your toddler reacts to his sibling the first time they meet isn't an indication of their future relationship – toddlers are very fickle and it simply depends on his mood.

CHILD ☺

Most children are very excited about meeting a new baby sibling. But even if things seem to be going well, try to keep your child 'in the loop'. For example, you could say, 'I think your baby sister is hungry.' This is obviously better than cooing at your baby, asking if she's hungry and inadvertently ignoring your older child.

From about the age of 3, your child can 'hold' the baby if he's sitting and supervised. If he doesn't want to, don't force it – he's most likely a bit afraid, or wants your attention all to himself.

If he wants to hold the baby, take this opportunity to tell him that he mustn't ever carry her, explaining how fragile babies are and how we mustn't risk dropping them. This doesn't guarantee that he won't ever try, so take care not to leave him unsupervised with the baby.

Try to resist asking your child questions about what he thinks of his new sibling. Of course you'll be keen for him to react in a positive way. But questions will put him under pressure to respond positively, which he may resent.

HOUSEKEEPING

Forget about this – you've just had a baby. Right now, your only responsibility is to look after yourself and your baby. There's no need to feel guilty about any of the following:

- Eating ready meals and takeaways
- Your eldest eating unhealthy snacks
- Unopened post
- Piles of dirty washing
- Stuff on the floor

- Grubby bathroom
- Cluttered kitchen
- Failing to reply to messages from family and friends (phone and email).

TROUBLESHOOTING

My child isn't interested in the baby

This is a common reaction and nothing to worry about. Your child is probably disappointed in how boring his new sibling is – after all, new babies don't do much more than sleep, feed, poo and cry. But as the baby starts to smile (at 6 weeks) and respond to your child, he'll no doubt become more interested. In the meantime, be patient – you've got years and years of magical moments ahead of you as you watch your children interact. Don't try to speed up this process – tempting though it may be – play with your eldest and chat about things that do interest him.

I've got too much milk and my baby keeps choking

This can sometimes happen if your children are closely spaced. It's as though your body is producing milk for a bigger baby and your newborn struggles with the fast flow of the milk. This will settle down after a week or so as your baby requires more milk, but in the meantime place your baby in a more upright position when you feed her to reduce spluttering. You can also try 'catching' the milk in a clean dry cloth at the beginning of a feed, when milk flow can be fastest. Avoid pumping your milk, as this will increase the flow further, and always let your baby have a break as soon as she starts to protest by fussing and wriggling.

CHAPTER 4
The First Week

You'll probably get lots of help this week, as your partner may have a week off work and perhaps your mum or mother-in-law may come to stay. There may also be visitors, cards, flowers and presents arriving – although perhaps not as many as with your first baby. But nonetheless, you'll all feel euphoric as you celebrate the arrival of your new baby and the fact that your family is bigger and busier.

Your firstborn is likely to be happy and excited about the baby initially – jealousy usually doesn't kick in until children realize that the baby is here to stay and won't be going 'back again'. And your tiredness will be temporarily masked by excitement and happiness. So keep the champagne flowing and the camera handy while you enjoy your new baby honeymoon high, and make as much use as you can of all the extra help offered.

MUM

With two children you'll no doubt welcome all the help you can get. But sometimes this can mean that you don't feel as close to your toddler or older child because he's likely to be taken off your hands to give you time with your baby. Don't worry too much about this as he'll be having a wonderful time with everyone else and will no doubt let you know if he's not happy.

But what you can do is to try to have a bit of bonding time each day with just the two of you, even if it's only 10 or 15 minutes. And you could get him involved with 'looking after' the baby so that he feels included – more on this on pages 45–46.

Take advantage of time alone with your baby to get breastfeeding established – it takes up to an hour to feed a newborn, who may well be hungry again an hour later. And do try to rest. Getting some sleep during the day is ideal, but sitting in bed feeding your baby is also more restful than being downstairs with everyone. So take yourself off at least once a day – you've only just given birth so keep reminding yourself that this is your week to recover from the birth.

It may be tempting to show off a bit to prove how well you are coping – after all, the birth was probably easier than last time, looking after a newborn seems like a doddle so far, and even being awake at night doesn't seem like such a big deal as previously. But take it from us, if you've got help you'd be foolish not to make the most of it – so sleep, rest, recover, read – be as 'lazy' as you want. You're going to have ample opportunity to show how well you are coping, probably from next week.

The baby blues usually kick in on about day 5, and this may hit harder than with your first baby as you're likely to be more tired and stressed. But it does pass quite quickly, usually within a day or two.

We mentioned in Chapter 1 the advantages of having either two boys or two girls. And any disappointment you may feel will almost certainly be softened by having a new baby in your arms. But you will still need to contend with comments from others such as, 'Oh, two girls, will you try for a boy?' 'Are you disappointed?' Or, 'I was so hoping for a granddaughter. Are you going to have any more?' This is the absolute last thing you want to hear – especially as you're almost certainly still sore from having just given birth. But try to resist giving a cutting response – if the culprit is trying to be spiteful, snapping back will only give them the satisfaction of knowing that they've got to you. But it's far more likely that they are simply being clumsy and socially inept. So give a bland response such as, 'They'll have such fun together as they grow up,' and hopefully it won't be mentioned again.

Finally, remember to do your pelvic floor exercises. If you got away with 'forgetting' to do them with your first baby, you are less likely to with your second.

Breastfeeding

If you breastfed your last baby then your milk may come in a day or so earlier than before and there may be a better supply. You'll also know what you're doing this time. But do be aware that sore nipples tend to recur, so if you suffered last time do take care how your baby latches on. With your last baby you probably got to the stage when you were able to latch your baby on effortlessly. Your baby would have learned what to do and also, by about month 2, babies' mouths are much bigger so they find it easier to latch on.

But with a newborn you need to be careful again, and it's important to take the time to position your baby correctly on your nipple when you feed her. Because a newborn's mouth is very small you can become sore quickly if she's not latched on properly and her gums rub your nipple. Although your midwife will no doubt tell you that you must focus carefully on latching your baby on correctly, it's also true that your nipples 'toughen up' after 2 to 3 weeks, so hang on in there – the pain will pass, just as it did last time.

Mastitis can also happen in the early days before your milk settles because you're more likely to get a blocked milk duct if you're not being super-vigilant when feeding. So ensure that your baby has completely finished on one breast before switching. And if you get a blocked milk duct – a sore, hard patch on your breast – take the time to unblock it to prevent it becoming infected and turning into mastitis. Sometimes it's just a matter of letting your baby suck for a little longer, even if it's uncomfortable – expressing milk can also work. And for a particularly stubborn duct, you can try a hot bath (as hot as you can bear) then massage and squeeze your breast to unblock the duct. You'll know when it's unblocked because it will suddenly feel less painful. This can take time, so lock the bathroom door and let others deal with your children for half an hour. If your blocked duct persists for longer than 24 hours, see your doctor. He or she will probably prescribe antibiotics.

Lots of mums who breastfed their first baby don't manage with their second. Although we give lots of tips throughout the book on coping with your eldest while you breastfeed, we know the reality can be very tough. So if you end up mixed feeding or exclusively bottle-feeding, try not to feel guilty.

This can be particularly hard because you'll no doubt worry that you're not giving your children an equal start in life. Well, it's impossible to give each of your children the same start, and there are actually plenty of benefits to being a second child. For a start, parents are better at reading their needs. Also, from the moment they are born, second babies will be handled and held in a more skilful and soothing way than first-borns. The list goes on, but the important message is not to feel bad about bottle-feeding – after all babies thrive on formula milk.

BABY

During this week your baby won't be in any sort of routine, which can be quite a relief in some ways as she'll just have to fit in with the family. She'll be feeding constantly – and of course it's essential to feed her on demand as she's so young, even if she wants milk every hour. She'll also be napping on and off around the clock, and needing lots of nappy changes a day (newborns poo up to 12 times every 24 hours).

It's also worth keeping a nappy-changing kit downstairs (or nearby). This will reduce the likelihood of you inadvertently delaying changing your baby's nappy – easily done if your toddler needs lots of attention. But it's important to change a new baby's nappy frequently to help avoid nappy rash.

Newborns fall asleep effortlessly so you can let your baby nap in her Moses basket in the corner of the living room. If she's with the family during the day, she'll not only learn to sleep through noise, but will start to become aware of the difference between day and night. Subsequent babies tend to learn this more quickly than first babies simply because the household is so much noisier and busier during the day than at night. But in the meantime, wakeful nights with your baby can be a wonderful bonding opportunity while everyone else sleeps. You'll probably find that this is one of the few times when you and your baby can gaze at each other, uninterrupted. And your eldest is fast asleep so won't get jealous.

First Bath

Your baby will probably have her first bath this week. This isn't essential if you are top and tailing her, and could wait until a couple of weeks if you choose. But if you do decide to bath her, this is a lovely activity to get your eldest involved in. Bathing your baby can be done at any time of the day, as it's too early to worry about a bath and bedtime routine. Half an hour after a feed works well if your baby is still awake – her bath need only take a couple of minutes and there's no need to use soap or baby shampoo; water is fine for now.

You can set up a baby bath in the bathroom and give your eldest a face cloth so that he can 'wash' the baby's feet – this will keep him away from her head. And while he's busy doing that, you can wash the rest of the baby. You could also let him pour a plastic cup of warm water over your baby's tummy while you hold her.

Do explain in advance to your eldest that the baby may hate her first bath and cry a lot (it can take some babies a few weeks to start to enjoy their bath).

Your child may be curious about the baby's genitals – this is very natural, especially if the baby is a different sex. Let him have a look, and talk about how girls and boys are different. Answer any questions he may have about the different sex organs as simply and honestly as you can.

It's also time to decide what you are going to call your baby's 'bits'. For boys, 'willy' is the obvious choice. Although 'penis' is the anatomically correct term, other children may not understand it. Likewise 'urethra' (the opening from which urine comes) is anatomically correct for girls, but unlikely to be understood by most children. So you may want to opt for something more childish such as 'front bottom' or 'wee hole' – choose something that you and your partner are comfortable with.

Your toddler will also be interested, and perhaps anxious, about your baby's cord stump and plastic clamp. You can reassure him and explain how this seals off the umbilical cord and how the baby got her food and oxygen via the cord when she was in your womb. There's nothing like a practical biology lesson! Don't panic too much if your toddler manages to touch the cord stump – it is far less sensitive than it looks.

TIP FOR ESTABLISHING A ROUTINE

There may be lots of visitors this week, most of whom will be delighted for your new baby to sleep in their arms – newborns sleep for up to 20 hours a day. But do ensure that she has a couple of naps in her Moses basket a day so that she doesn't become dependent on being held when she sleeps. At this age, this is all you need to do as far as a routine is concerned.

TODDLER 🄰🄱🄲

Most toddlers rather enjoy the excitement of a new baby – there's so much going on with all the extra visitors and Dad being around that, ironically, they barely notice their new sibling.

Let your toddler be in charge of opening any gifts that visitors may bring for the baby – explain that the baby is too young to open her own presents so needs her big brother to help. Opening the presents and being allowed to 'play' with them should quell any potential jealousy, and he's quite likely to dismiss the presents as 'boring'. If he happens to want to keep one of the gifts for himself, then go along with it. Chances are, if nobody's that bothered he'll soon become tired of it. And if he's determined to keep it for himself, then let him. It's not that big a deal if the baby has one less cuddly toy – your toddler obviously needs reassurance that he's not second-best after the baby. So allow him his mini-rebellion.

Your toddler's usual routine will probably fall apart a bit this week as he 'gets away with' eating endless biscuits then picking at his meals, and having countless bedtime stories and going to bed late. You'll no doubt be stressing about this as you watch all your hard work being undone. But don't worry too much because it will be relatively quick to get your toddler back into his good habits once the excitement of the new baby has subsided, Dad's back at work and Granny has gone home. It takes 3 or 4 days to re-establish routines so we suggest that 4 days before your first day on your own with the two children, you bath your toddler and put him to bed yourself to get him back into old patterns. If possible have the baby around too, perhaps being looked after by Dad, to show your toddler that he can still have his special time with Mum before he goes to sleep even if the baby is there.

Your toddler may not yet realize that the baby is here to stay and won't disappear once all the excitement is over. Gently explain if this issue arises, but allow time for your toddler to understand the concept – suddenly having a new sibling is a big life event. But before long he probably won't be able to remember not having a sibling.

CHILD

Your child will hopefully be very interested in his new sibling this week, so try to include him whenever possible and give him as much responsibility as you dare. During her bath you could hold the baby while he washes her with a face cloth. Explain that the baby is very slippery so you'll need his help, and with any luck he'll rise to the challenge.

He may also enjoy choosing an outfit for the baby to wear, rubbing her back to soothe her if she's crying (you'll be holding the baby for this), or doing the poppers up on her sleepsuit. Let him make faces at the baby – he'll have to get close, as your baby won't be able to see further than 30cm (1ft) away. And ask your child for advice – 'Why is the baby crying, I've just fed her, has she got wind, is she tired?' Strangely, young children can be uncannily perceptive about their siblings, so you may get the right answer. But even if he hasn't got a clue, your child will feel valued by the fact that you asked his opinion.

And when you're with your child and the baby starts crying, you can roll your eyes and even confide that you're getting a bit fed up with all the crying and feeding. Your child will get the message that you and him are in it together looking after this demanding newborn, and this will help him to feel involved and important.

This is infinitely better than being snugly bound together with your baby, with your older child very much the outsider. Your child is very sensitive and liable to jealousy, whereas your baby is far too young to become jealous – she'll be happy as long as she's fed. So make the most of this and 'favour' your eldest child while you can. Obviously you won't be able to continue this 'favouritism' as your baby gets older, but right now it will help to lay down a good foundation of your eldest feeling secure and loved despite the arrival of a new sibling. And the more secure children feel, the easier they find it to be nice to their siblings.

It's also important to reminisce with your child about what it was like when he was a baby. Keep your stories positive to show that he too was a very loved and treasured baby, and perhaps dig out some photos or videos.

BUILDING THE SIBLING BOND

When it comes to asking your child to help with the baby, always remember that your aim is to build up the bond between your child and baby, not to use him as free help. Helping with the baby should always be seen as optional fun, not a chore. So accept it if your child doesn't want to get involved. It's one thing to insist that a 7-year-old lays the table, but children shouldn't be forced to help with younger siblings, as they are likely to become resentful.

HOUSEKEEPING

You'll no doubt have visits from family and friends this week, and don't forget that the midwife will be popping in, too. Don't worry if you happen to be in your dressing gown when your visitors arrive – this will actually stop people staying too long and crush any expectation of being given a meal. And forget the mess – if you empty the kitchen bin and squirt a bit of bleach down the toilet from time to time, then at least your home won't smell. Everything else can wait.

Now that you've got more than one child, you really will have your hands full, so we suggest that you make the most of your visitors and get them to help – most of them will be delighted to. Here are some jobs you can ask visitors to help with, and jobs you can't.

You can ask visitors to:

- Hold the baby
- Hold the toddler, play with him and read to him (though be prepared for him to object if he doesn't know the person well)
- Put flowers into vases

- Make tea and coffee
- Find biscuits
- Open wine.

If visitors offer to help you can ask them to:

- Help your eldest with his meal (again, this works better if he knows them well)
- Play with your eldest (if he doesn't get enough attention from visitors, he's likely to misbehave)
- Fold clean washing – if it belongs to the baby or your toddler (small, sweet clothes) and happens to be in a basket downstairs so that the visitors don't have to go off on their own like servants
- Order a takeaway (tell them where your money is so they don't think they're expected to pay)
- Wash up if they've eaten the meal – don't ask them to do your washing up from previous meals.

Don't ask visitors to do the following:

- Change your toddler's pooey nappy
- Any cleaning jobs
- Upstairs jobs – visitors won't want to feel isolated.

Residential Visitors

It's offensive to ask your mother or mother-in-law or whoever else is staying to tidy up or clean, but you can certainly ask them to help with the baby and toddler. There are dozens of very pleasant jobs you can suggest they do, such as bathing the baby or toddler, reading stories, soothing the baby and making lunch for your eldest (they may even be willing to prepare the evening meal if cooking's their thing). Our big tip is to play to their strengths and ask them to do the things they love. If they happen to be the bossy, capable type, then allow them to be 'in charge' – it may be annoying but it's also very useful for you to be able to rest, and it won't last for long.

Fill Your Diary

While you've got the extra help this week, find some time to get some dates in your diary for your first week on your own, particularly your first day. You and your toddler may already have a busy weekly timetable and you'll hopefully be able to continue with these activities along with your newborn. But if you've only recently stopped work, then ask around and find some local playgroups. You could also arrange to see antenatal friends who may also have just had their second baby – this is a very pleasant way to spend time if your older child is at school.

TROUBLESHOOTING

My mother-in-law is driving me crazy but I don't know how I'll cope when she's gone

The mother-in-law relationship is quite complex, and problems tend to stem from an underlying power struggle. From your point of view, it's your children, your home and your husband, whereas she perceives that it's her grandchildren and her son – and, most importantly, she's had infinitely more experience. So there's often underlying tension. This is exacerbated by sleep deprivation and the fact that your mother-in-law is staying with you. However tetchy or critical she may be, keep reminding yourself that she's there to spend time with her grandchildren and to help out.

So ask her to look after the children for a couple of hours so that you can get some extra sleep. Not only will you feel less resentful about her being around if she's really helping you, you'll also feel much better once you've had a bit of sleep. And she'll hopefully enjoy being on her own with the children and proving just how well she can manage. If you thank her and compliment her on how well she copes, you'll probably get a lovely long sleep every day. Don't expect her to do everything perfectly – you may well emerge from your sleep to discover that the baby's nappy needs changing and your toddler has been eating biscuits all morning. But bite your tongue, because extra sleep is far more satisfying than point-scoring.

CHAPTER 5
The First Day on Your Own

The first day on your own doesn't mean bundling your children into the car and driving for 2 hours to spend the day with your sister. Of course, it's important to spend lots of time with supportive relatives and friends in the early weeks and months. But there will also be times when they're not around. So in this chapter we give you an hour-by-hour timetable to help you through the first day and beyond when it's just you and your children.

With any luck, your partner will either get your eldest up and dressed in the morning before he goes to work, or will be home early enough to help with bathtime – and if you're really lucky, he'll do both.

But to ensure that this chapter is as helpful as possible, we're going to assume that you don't get any help from Dad – perhaps he leaves for work very early and returns very late, is working abroad, or you may be single.

We found that it's actually easier to be quite regimented at this stage, rather than going with the flow – there's plenty of time for being more laid-back in the coming months and years. So we've introduced a plan to help you structure your day. Careful planning and organization mean that you can get through some parts of the day on auto-pilot – essential if you've only had a few hours' sleep.

We're going to suggest that you follow a daily pattern of getting up and out reasonably early in the morning, then come home for lunch, naps and quiet play before tea and bedtime. This is how most mums looking after two or more small children on their own seem to cope best.

Keeping your eldest child in his own routine, especially if he's still a toddler, should be a priority because if he's happy, the day will go reasonably smoothly. So plan your day around him rather than your baby, who is young enough to fit in with whatever's happening as she's still too young to be in a routine at this stage. Just ensure she's well fed. You'll find that she'll naturally start to fall into the 'family routine' over the coming weeks – and we'll be talking more about this in the forthcoming chapters.

When writing this daily plan, we assumed that your child doesn't yet go to nursery or school, or indeed have any kind of childcare. But if your child is older and goes to school or nursery, this plan will still be helpful because it spells out how to get up, dressed and out of the house, as well as how to cope with two children at bath- and bedtime. We've included more detailed information about managing the nursery or school run in the 'Child' section (on pages 56–57).

MUM

The first day on your own with both children is the day that many mums dread. It can seem rather daunting, yet with a bit of planning you'll not only manage the day but hopefully enjoy it, too.

Our big tip is not to do anything too ambitious. We all get tempted to prove how well we are coping by baking cupcakes or getting the paints out. But your toddler will almost certainly be just as happy with pretend plastic food or colouring pencils, which are less messy and don't require constant supervision.

If your eldest is at school or nursery, you may well choose to simply relish the time at home alone with your baby – you'll probably find that you enjoy your second baby more than your first because you know what you are doing, and time on your own together will seem like a luxury rather than a stressful challenge. Of course the school run will be more hectic now that you've got a baby, but nothing you can't cope with – more on this later.

Breastfeeding

New babies feed very slowly and breastfeeding can take up to an hour. This can be a nightmare if you've also got a demanding toddler to look after. Here are some coping strategies, each with advantages and disadvantages. We suggest that at each feed you select the one most suited to your toddler's mood and the time of day. Used in combination, you'll avoid too many pitfalls.

1. **Give your toddler a snack.**

    Pros: Snack food is distracting and will soothe a distraught toddler instantly.

    Cons: Your toddler may end up eating too much between meals, then fuss when it's time to sit and eat proper food. And he may start to expect a snack every time you feed the baby.

2. **Have a box of special toys set aside just for when you are feeding your baby.**

    Also, you can buy a child's table and chair set: some children will play particularly well by themselves while sitting at these (they are too small for adults to sit at, so they give children a sense of territory and also importance).

    Pros: Playing alone is a calming and creative way for your toddler to spend time, and you'll feel like an excellent mum.

    Cons: This won't work for all toddlers and won't work every day, in which case you need a back-up plan. And it takes time and organization to keep the box stocked up.

3. **Television.**

   Pros: This is instant, takes no effort and will hold your toddler's attention long enough for you to be able to feed your baby.

   Cons: Too much television has been shown to be detrimental to young children, especially the under-2s who, in an ideal world, should never watch television. Also your baby may finish her feed just as a new programme begins – stick to short programmes or record the programme 'to watch later'. If you watch television together, you can always chat about the characters afterwards to boost language skills.

4. **Encourage your toddler to 'feed' his favourite toy.**

   It's actually quite common for toddlers to put their toys under their tops to breastfeed, or even to be pregnant (boys as well as girls!).

   Pros: Your toddler will feel important and involved.

   Cons: This won't hold his attention for long.

5. **Be his audience.**

   Toddlers relish an audience, and this is easy to do while sitting and feeding. Simply comment on what he's doing – 'What a big boy! You can climb onto the sofa, jump off again and climb on again.'

   Pros: This may buy you a few precious minutes at the end of a feed.

   Cons: It won't work every time.

THE TELEVISION DEBATE

Television can be extremely useful in these early days. Critics will say that you're using it as a babysitter, but frankly, if you're looking after a newborn and another child, you *need* a babysitter. So don't feel guilty, just be sensible and limit television to the times you're struggling, such as getting dressed, breastfeeding or preparing dinner.

BABY

By the second week your baby will be more aware of her surroundings and won't sleep quite as effortlessly as when she was newborn. She'll need a bit more rocking and soothing than initially and she'll also wake more easily if she hears a noise, most likely your toddler. But she'll soon become used to his noise and learn to sleep through it – there's little point in trying to keep him quiet.

As for feeding, your baby will go slightly longer between feeds – around 3 hours generally. But do look out for the 3-week growth spurt (around day 19) when your baby will want to feed almost constantly for about 2 days. If this happens to occur on your first day alone with your baby and child, being aware of it and knowing that it will come to an end very soon will be a comfort. In the meantime it's just a matter of getting through as best you can.

Use a baby sling as much as possible. This will not only make life easier when you have another child, but evidence suggests that carried babies are happier. So throughout this chapter we suggest wearing a sling when you are at home, as this frees you up to do other things, mainly looking after your eldest. Wearing a sling when you go out is also useful; it's easier to chase after a wayward toddler than if you had to push a buggy. And when you bump into friends, they won't be able to make too much fuss of a baby snuggled in a sling, which is helpful for your toddler who may be easily jealous at this time.

TIPS FOR ESTABLISHING A ROUTINE

Start to nudge your baby towards feeding more during the day than at night by taking particular care when winding her during the day, as this will enable her to take in more milk. A shortcut is to keep her in a baby sling – if she's upright, she'll probably burp.

TODDLER 🄰🄱🄲

The key to managing a baby and a toddler is to tire your toddler out in the morning so that he sleeps better during his afternoon nap, if he still has one, or at least is more content to play quietly if he's grown out of his daily nap. This will enable you to have a break.

Our favourite morning activity is playgroup, because your toddler will be safe and able to run around. And there will be other mums there to keep an eye on him, hold your baby if necessary and, of course, chat to.

Do note that toddlers like the pace to be very slow, so whenever possible try not to rush. For example, this is the time to master pushing the buggy one-handed, while using your other hand to help your toddler balance along a wall. By being patient you'll actually save more time in the end because the slow pace will keep your toddler calmer than if you hurry and he kicks off and has a tantrum.

Another way to keep your toddler calm is to ensure that you listen to him and make eye contact. It's surprisingly easy to forget these basic skills when you're simultaneously struggling to mend a train set, rock a cranky baby and wondering what you're going to give everyone for dinner. But listening carefully to your toddler will mean he's less likely to become frustrated and so play up in order to get attention.

CHILD 😀

An older child will be at school or nursery during the day, which most mums agree makes life easier when you have a baby. But the downside is having to do the school run. Do let the school or nursery know that you've just had a baby in case you are ever late, but also allow lots of time.

However organized you are or however much time you allow, it's almost impossible not to be late occasionally when you have a newborn, because babies are so unpredictable.

The obvious answer is to ask for help – people like to help and you may well find another mum who is more than willing to pick your child up from time to time and take him to school.

And for the days when you are on your own and getting ready to leave, we've written some guidelines on when to leave the house and when to be late.

Leave the House if...

- Your baby starts grizzling because she's becoming hungry and you know you can feed her within the next 15 minutes – in the car outside the school gates after you've dropped your child off, if necessary.

Don't Leave the House if...

- She does a poo and she has nappy rash. This condition can become worse within a few hours, so it's important to stop and change her nappy or she could end up with extremely red, raw skin.
- She does a poo that squelches up her back to her neck. There's no need to stop and bath her – you can do this when you get back. But you will need to clean her up with wipes and change her clothes.

Even more important than dropping your child off on time is not being late to pick him up. So don't be tempted to let your baby finish napping if it means cutting things fine. If you wake her at the same time each day for the school run, she'll soon adapt her routine.

When you see your child, give him an especially warm greeting and don't expect him to be in the least bit interested in what you and the baby have been doing. The only exception may be a particularly grisly baby poo story, which most young children will find amusing.

HOUSEKEEPING

We've suggested that you manage your time by having a busy morning, perhaps taking your toddler and baby to playgroup, and then have a quiet afternoon. This plan is very easy to adapt for when you need to get your chores done.

For example, you can go to the post office, doctor's or shops first thing, then afterwards you can still go along to playgroup – a good opportunity to feed your baby. A café is another option if you need to feed your baby, or perhaps visit the local park on your way home – alfresco breastfeeding is something many mums of two soon learn.

The idea is that you get yourself organized and only have to go out once a day rather than twice. Then you'll only have to endure 'leaving the house' once.

TROUBLESHOOTING

I can't even pop out to buy a paper anymore because it takes 40 minutes to get out of the door with the little ones

It's quite common to feel a bit trapped and housebound in the early days, which is why we suggest getting out each morning. But if you do need to go out again later, then here are some shortcuts. Take the double buggy, if you've got one, and plan your trip around your toddler's snack time – if you promise your toddler that he can have raisins in the buggy, he'll no doubt co-operate and will happily climb in. And forget about getting your toddler 'ready'. If you're only going to be out for 20 minutes there's no need to worry about shoes, or even socks if it's a warm day. You certainly won't be the only mum taking such shortcuts – just look around and you'll start to notice plenty of shoeless, snack-munching toddlers in buggies. Of course you'll need to ensure that your baby has a clean nappy and isn't due for a feed. But you'll find it much easier getting one child 'ready' rather than two.

My partner and I have always enjoyed dinner together once our eldest is in bed. But now I feel too exhausted

Life will start to settle down again in a couple of months as your baby starts to go to bed at the same time as your toddler, which will give you back your evenings. She'll also have stopped feeding constantly and will be much easier to look after. In the meantime you need to prioritize sleep above quality time with your partner – the less tired you are, the less snappy you will be, so it's better at this stage to have eggs on toast and an early night than a long sit-down meal with your partner. If you both understand that it's only for a couple of months, it will be easier to accept. Having a new baby and another child is very tough and you need to get into the mindset of survival and not rush getting things back to the way they were.

24-HOUR SURVIVAL PLAN

The following 24-hour plan will help you get through your first day alone with your children, and also through the days and weeks to come.

The Night Before

One of the best ways of getting organized is to spend about 15 minutes every evening before you go to bed preparing for the next day. So find shoes, coats, pack the nappy bag, charge your phone, find your keys and get rid of any dirty nappies or rubbish from the buggy. It's worth tidying your hall each day, because this is where stress can really build if you can't find shoes and so on when you're trying to leave.

You can also get clothes out for yourself and your children for the next morning, locate toys for your toddler (things he particularly likes or something he's not played with for a while – these will keep him occupied), plan the next day's meals, write your shopping list and set up a downstairs nappy-changing area if you haven't done so already. This will mean you don't have to disturb your toddler every time your baby needs her nappy changed.

You'll feel exhausted in the evenings and be tempted to postpone these chores until the next day, but believe us, it's worth making an effort to get ahead, because doing any of these tasks the next day will take much longer. And if you're having to run upstairs and search for nappies with two crying children waiting in the hall, it will not only take longer but be very stressful.

If your baby is unsettled in the evenings, you can actually do these things while she's in the baby sling.

Getting Up

Your first day on your own will begin with the challenge of getting out of bed. It's quite likely that your baby kept you up much of the night, then wakes you for her final feed at around 6 a.m. This will take up to an hour, and by the time you've changed her nappy (she'll still be pooing after nearly every feed at this age) and settled her, your toddler will be awake.

When your partner or someone else was around they could look after your toddler while you went back to sleep – but there's no such luxury when you're on your own.

Our tip is to have an indulgent treat to look forward to – a sit-down and a cup of tea once you've got everyone dressed, or a sneaky piece of chocolate while you prepare your toddler's breakfast. And plan a rest for later in the day – simply knowing that you're going to get a break will instantly make you feel a little less exhausted and hopefully help you to drag yourself out of bed – despite feeling almost beyond tiredness.

Having one or two planned treats during the day will help get you through the early weeks.

Getting Dressed

Mum

Once you're up, your next challenge will be showering and getting dressed. Don't put this off or you'll still be in your pyjamas at 11 a.m. – not good for morale.

While you shower you can keep your toddler occupied by giving him a book or toy he hasn't seen for a while. Rotating toys is extremely effective for all children, particularly so in the under-3s because young children's short-term memory isn't very developed. This means your toddler will respond as though he's been given something brand new. Plan this in advance (the night before) rather than dashing about in the morning trying to find something suitable.

If your baby is asleep, lock her in your room in her Moses basket or cot – she'll be safe because she won't be moving yet, and also your toddler won't be able to get to her. If she's awake, put her in a bouncy chair in the corner of the bathroom. Before the age of 2 months she won't be able to see particularly clearly, but she will enjoy lights, reflections and movement from birth. And she'll find the different acoustics in the bathroom and the sound of running water interesting, too.

Keep the bathroom door open or your toddler may become anxious. If he wanders in to see you, have a bath toy handy to pass to him – this should distract him long enough for you to rinse off before he starts trying to play with the baby.

You'll have to be quick in the shower, and if you're washing your hair, you won't necessarily get a chance to dry it – if you happen to get a few minutes, start with the front in case you have to stop before you're finished.

As for makeup – it takes less than a minute to put on tinted moisturizer and mascara but you'll still feel slightly smug for an entire day, so it's worth the small effort.

Take your clothes with you into the bathroom so that you can (hopefully) get dressed quickly before your toddler notices – once you leave the bathroom, you'll almost certainly find that he starts making demands. Likewise with your baby: if you move her bouncy chair into the bedroom she may start to grizzle and want you to pick her up.

An alternative to a morning shower is an evening bath when your children are asleep – this will be easier once your baby is about 3 months and goes to bed early.

Baby

Your baby will probably still be wearing sleepsuits most of the time, but if you are going to get her 'dressed', do so during her first early morning nappy change. She'll be half-undressed anyway, and also awake. Then keep a bib on her during feeds in case she brings up any milk – this will save you having to change her outfit.

Toddler

If your toddler is still in nappies you can get him dressed when you change his night nappy, when he will be half-undressed.

Breakfast

Once you're all dressed, you can have breakfast – it's quicker to get everyone dressed before breakfast than afterwards because there's less running up and down stairs – or rushing between different rooms.

You can either put your baby in a bouncy chair while you and your toddler have breakfast, or you may have to feed her simultaneously – your baby is still a bit unpredictable at this stage. When your toddler has finished eating he'll probably be happy enough to play for a little while before you go out – most toddlers play well at this time because they're not tired or hungry and are looking forward to going out.

This will give you a chance to clear away breakfast and feed your baby should she need another feed at this time. Alternatively you can race off to playgroup where you can breastfeed your baby, and leave any clearing up until later.

Leaving the House

Make sure your baby has had a feed within the hour you intend to leave, and change her nappy as near to leaving as possible. This will help to reduce the chance of her getting nappy rash, caused by urine being broken down by bacteria in poo to form ammonia, which burns the skin. The drier your baby's nappy when she poos, the less urine will be present to release ammonia. So if she happens to poo 5 minutes after you've left home, nappy rash will hopefully be less of a problem, although do stop and change her as soon as you can.

When it's time to go out, get your baby ready first as she'll be slightly more patient than your toddler, and more inclined to wait while you get your eldest ready. Once your baby is in outdoor clothes, put your own coat on, then put her into her baby sling (or strap her into her buggy if you're not using a sling). If she's a bit grizzly or crying – and you are confident the reason isn't hunger or real distress – there's no point wasting time trying to calm her, just get out as quickly as you can because she's probably just tired and you'll find that she falls asleep once you set off.

You can start to get your toddler ready once your baby is in her sling, or strapped in her buggy. If your hall is organized and you've already located shoes and coats, this will be quick. Ideally he will put on his own shoes and coat, but don't make too much of an issue about this – he'll see you fussing over the baby and may crave such fuss and attention for himself and want you to get him ready, even if he previously could do it himself. He'll find it quite distressing if you refuse because he'll think you love the baby more than him.

Playgroup

If your eldest is still a toddler then we particularly recommend going to playgroup (or perhaps library story time, or other mum-and-tot activity) in the morning to allow your eldest to run around while you feed your baby. It will also give you some adult company – we can't recommend this enough in the early days. However exhausted you feel, there's something very uplifting and reassuring in having a chat with other mums.

When you arrive at playgroup, a friend's house or other activity, do try to make your toddler rather than the baby the star of the show. This is particularly easy if your baby is asleep in the sling. If your toddler gets lots of attention it will help him go off and play happily by himself. And if your baby is awake, you can say to her, 'Baby, let's watch your big brother, he's going to ride on the tractor'... and so on. This should also encourage your toddler to go off and play.

But don't be surprised if he wants to cling to you instead. Give him lots of cuddles and let him stay with you until he decides he wants to play. If he is clingy, then trying to persuade him to go off before he feels ready will actually make him cling for longer. And do make the most of the fact that there will be lots of willing volunteers desperate to hold your baby while you play with your toddler.

It's quite common for toddlers with new siblings to misbehave and bash or push other children – an instant way of diverting your attention away from the baby and onto them. Making your toddler feel like the star of the show will help to prevent this from happening in the first place. So be constantly aware of your toddler and keep admiring and praising what he does. Walk over with the baby to see him from time to time. And try to 'ignore' your baby – it's particularly important when you're out not to coo at your baby, because other people will make a tremendous fuss of a newborn. When they do, you can say quietly to your toddler, 'Everyone likes your baby sister/brother, don't they?', to keep him feeling special and involved, too.

You'll also need to keep check of how much you chat to the other mothers – don't get so involved in conversation that you lose track of what your toddler is up to. By all means have a chat; you'll no doubt relish the adult company. But while your baby is still so new, ensure that you keep giving your toddler plenty of attention; then he's far less likely to misbehave.

Try to take the opportunity to feed your baby and change his nappy while out. If your toddler is occupied you'll have a little time. Being out can be a great opportunity for a long feed for your baby.

Lunch

When you arrive home, keep your baby in her sling while you prepare lunch for you and your toddler. If she needs feeding, you can do this while your toddler has his lunch. Don't worry if you have to keep her waiting 10 minutes – though it will seem like an eternity as she howls in red-faced outrage, it won't do her any harm. And after a few days she'll start to learn when 'lunch time' is as she adapts her body clock a few minutes to fit in with the family.

Have lunch planned, and choose something quick to prepare – sandwiches or eggs, for instance. It's bad enough if your toddler is crying from hunger and tiredness, but if your baby is crying as well this can seem utterly overwhelming and you won't be able to think straight, let alone make decisions. Knowing in advance what you're making for lunch will be a huge help. The only way out of this situation is to get both children fed as quickly as possible. (See Chapter 6 for more on coping when both children are crying.)

It is just about possible to breastfeed a baby and feed a toddler in a high chair at the same time (especially if your toddler has lots of finger foods to eat).

Alternatively you can feed your baby after your toddler's lunch if she's happy to wait – she may well be asleep in her sling or pram when you arrive home if you managed to feed her at playgroup.

After-lunch Nap

After lunch, put your toddler down for his usual nap. If possible, leave your baby in her Moses basket while you do this so that your toddler gets your undivided attention, but if she's fussing then pop her into the sling to soothe her.

Clear up lunch – do it now because you probably won't want to get up again once you sit down. But don't get carried away with other chores, because you no doubt need to rest.

Your baby is still too young to have a long afternoon nap, so rather than wasting time and energy trying to get her to settle, you'd be better off slumping on the sofa together, probably for another feed. Read, watch daytime television, eat chocolate, answer emails or make a phone call – five things you can't do with a toddler but which are possible with a feeding or snoozing baby. A bit of self-indulgence at this time will help re-charge you for the rest of the day, which will be busy.

Do try to put your baby in her Moses basket whenever you can. This is particularly important if you're about to fall asleep, because there is a risk of cot death as babies have been known to suffocate in the soft cushions of sofas while their parents doze.

And there are several other advantages to putting her in the Moses basket. First, she'll be lying flat, which allows her to move freely and is good for back muscle development. Secondly, she'll learn to drop off to sleep by herself rather than become dependent on being in your arms. And finally, the Moses basket will stop her from becoming dependent on being held all the time. Having said that, demanding to be constantly held probably won't become an issue with your second baby – this is because you'll often be too busy with your older child to be able to pick her up as soon as she starts crying. Insisting on being carried 24 hours a day tends to be a luxury reserved for the first baby in the family.

Afternoon Play

When your toddler wakes you can put the baby's Moses basket into a playpen to prevent your toddler getting to her – she will still be near and able to let you know when she wants feeding.

If you put your baby in a bouncy chair, always strap her in. Although she's too young to be able to move enough to fall out, your toddler may bounce the chair or try to lift the baby out – but if she's strapped in this will buy you a few essential seconds to dash across the room and rescue her.

After nap time you'll have a couple of hours before dinner. Your toddler will want some one-to-one time with you, so try to give him some attention – ideally while your baby sleeps (again, put her into the sling if she's unsettled). It doesn't have to be anything elaborate – a story on your knee is fine, or perhaps giving teddy a pretend drink. Five minutes of one-to-one attention every now and again throughout the day will make your toddler feel more special than one mammoth cookery or painting session – and it will be a lot easier for you.

We mentioned bathing the baby together in the last chapter; this is not only a fun way to spend some time together but it will also make bathtime later on easier as you'll only be bathing one child and not two. You'll no doubt want to start introducing a bath- and bedtime routine to your baby before too long, but there's not much point yet when she's so young, especially on your first day on your own with the two of them.

Teatime

When it comes to feeding your toddler, opt for something you know he likes, so you avoid any mealtime battles – after all, it is your first day on your own. And choose something very easy – a pre-prepared frozen meal works well because you can pop it in the microwave, for example shepherd's pie and peas. Oven meals also work well, for example oven chips and fish fingers (and vegetables, too, of course!), because once it's in the oven you can forget about it for 15 minutes. Do use an oven timer – it's so easy to become distracted by your baby or toddler and for dinner to burn.

We suggest bulk cooking at weekends so that you've got plenty of instant meals for the week. But if you do need to spend a bit of time cooking, then half an hour's pre-dinner television for your toddler can help.

This will probably be the most fractious meal of the day, because both your baby and toddler will be tired, and of course you will be, too. So it's particularly important for you to remain calm. Ensure that you have everything you may need for the meal – drinks, cloths, kitchen paper, ketchup and so on. Then sit down with your toddler.

You may well choose to eat at this time – you'll no doubt be hungry if you've eaten breakfast and lunch with your toddler, even though this is probably a couple of hours earlier than you'd normally have your meals. But it can be difficult to remember to eat in these busy early weeks, and eating meals with your toddler is a simple solution. What's more, it sets an excellent example for your toddler to see you sitting down and eating the same food as him.

In weeks to come you could just have a cup of tea, then have an adult meal with your partner later. In Chapter 7 we'll be covering how to cook meals that your toddler can eat early and you and your partner can enjoy alone together later.

You may well have to feed the baby while your toddler eats. But most toddlers are happily absorbed while eating dessert, so this is an ideal time to breastfeed.

Leave clearing up until after the meal – if teatime is calm and you've given your toddler some attention, he'll probably play happily for 10 minutes afterwards while you clear up.

As for your baby, put her into her sling if she's fractious. But if she's calm she can lay in her Moses basket. And from about 6 weeks she will be happy to watch her older sibling play from her bouncy chair.

Bathtime and Bedtime

You'll only have to bath your toddler, as you've bathed your baby earlier. And even if you haven't, it's fine to just top and tail her.

From about 10 months toddlers have the core stability and strength to be able to sit up easily in the bath (the test is, can your child pull himself up to standing?). Once he is able to do this, he can play in the bath while you change your baby's nappy and put her in a fresh sleepsuit. For your toddler's safety never leave the bathroom, so bring the changing mat and everything you'll need into the bathroom before you put your toddler in the bath. Then sit your baby in a bouncy chair so that she can enjoy watching the action, or use the sling if she's fretful.

When it comes to bedtime stories, some toddlers will be happy to share your knee with the baby – after all, she won't be doing much yet to grab the attention during story-telling. But most toddlers would probably prefer it if the baby wasn't around, so ideally she can stay in her chair, or perhaps her Moses basket. You can even put her into your toddler's cot. At the very least, try to avoid breastfeeding your baby just before your toddler goes to bed – breastfeeding is very intimate and exclusive, so he may feel particularly upset because he'll think it should be him having special time on your knee.

If your baby does need a feed at this critical time and your toddler doesn't seem happy about it, tell him that he can have bonus stories until the end of her feed, and can still have his special 'Mummy time' after that. Lots of eye-rolling and telling him that you'd rather the baby didn't need feeding right now will also help to get him on your side.

Try to keep your toddler's bedtime routine as close as possible to what it was before the baby was born. And when you leave his room, don't let your toddler hear you talking to your baby because he'll feel excluded.

Ideally, feed your baby once you've settled your toddler. You'll have time for a long, uninterrupted feed, as well as a well-earned rest. You'll find that your toddler will pretty much dictate your baby's bedtime feeding pattern over the next few weeks. Either he'll be happy enough for you to feed her while you read him stories, in which case you'll soon be able to put her down to sleep at the same time your toddler goes to sleep. Or he'll be distraught when you feed her during 'his time', which will result in the feed being interrupted and unsatisfactory. If this is the case, your baby will gradually learn to wait until he's in bed; then she'll be able to have a long, peaceful feed.

Both of these routines work well – which one you end up following rather depends on the age and temperament of your toddler.

Once your toddler is settled you'll just be coping with your baby, which you'll no doubt find straightforward, having looked after two children all day. All we'd say is remember to get yourself organized for tomorrow. And if your baby allows you, have an early night.

CHAPTER 6
The Early Weeks: 1–6

The first 6 weeks is a particularly difficult period, because your baby will be feeding and pooing constantly and waking throughout the night. And of course having another child to look after will make things especially challenging.

In an ideal world your baby would be in a regular feeding and sleeping pattern that fitted neatly around your toddler's timetable. But right now your baby really is too young to be following a routine – you can start to think about this from around 6 weeks, and we'll be talking a lot more about routine in the next couple of chapters.

In the meantime, it's more a case of survival. Living in a state of chaos and mayhem is actually fairly normal at this stage, and if you can accept this rather than try to conquer it, you'll feel a lot less stressed. The other way to keep stress levels low is to know that your baby will develop and become a lot easier to look after within just a few weeks – so hang on in there.

In this chapter we give strategies and shortcuts that we've found helpful. And we give some simple steps to prevent either your baby or toddler getting into bad habits that will be difficult to break later.

One final word – although we've written this book to help mothers (or fathers) cope on their own with small children, we know that plenty of mums do manage to get a bit of childcare at some stage. If you're going to get any help, we'd strongly advise that you do so in these early weeks.

MUM

After the excitement of a new baby, tiredness will start to really take its toll – especially if you've little or no childcare. Do try to rest during the day and have early nights whenever possible – it's very easy to underestimate how tired you are. It's often only when we look back that we realize the extent of our exhaustion. Of course you'll need to keep up with a few essential chores, but if you add 'have a sleep' to your to-do list it will help you see it as a priority.

Eating regularly will also help to keep your energy levels up. You may find that you forget to eat because you're too busy. Or perhaps you nibble on biscuits all day, then don't feel great as a result. A better option is to eat with your eldest child whenever possible – not only will you be taking the time to sit down for a proper meal, you'll be setting him a good example and giving him plenty of attention, too. For his final meal of the day you could just have a cup of tea or perhaps serve yourself a portion of vegetables if you're planning to eat with your partner later. Remember to chop your food up before your meal, because you'll probably eat it one-handed while simultaneously breastfeeding your baby and spoon-feeding your toddler.

Lots of mums of two or more find these early weeks particularly overwhelming, and you may suddenly feel desperate for some extra help. The obvious solution is to get some childcare: sometimes as little as a few hours a week can make a difference. Alternatively you could get some domestic help. Whether you opt for someone to help with the children or a cleaner largely depends on what stresses you out more – looking after two children or the mess and muddle?

Here are some options:

1. Find someone to take both children to the park for a couple of hours. This will allow you to have some time to yourself and regain your sanity. And it's amazing how much you can get done when you're in the house on your own. We suggest that, before you start on your

chores, you lie down for a quick nap – if you end up sleeping for the whole time, you obviously needed it. Do ensure that the person looking after your children is experienced enough to give your toddler plenty of attention rather than fuss too much over the baby.

2. Arrange for someone to come to your home to help with teatime and bathtime. An extra pair of hands will make this busy period easier and more relaxed.

3. Employ a cleaner – even if it's just once a week, it will be a big psychological boost knowing that your entire home will soon be clean and tidy. And you could arrange for your cleaner to come more often, say every other day, so that she could take charge of the laundry as well as the cleaning.

4. If paid help isn't an option and you have no family nearby, you still have other options – your friends. Call them and admit that you're desperate. Your close childless friends may happily come over once or twice to help out – and if you invite them to come early enough they can help with bathtime. Then you can have some quiet time together once your toddler is in bed and you're just feeding the baby. You could even arrange your online-ordered grocery shopping to be delivered while your friends are there so that there will be someone to hold the baby while you unpack it. But do explain your intentions in advance, or it may seem a little odd when the delivery van suddenly arrives.

Of course practical help is important, but the psychological benefits of looking forward to the help shouldn't be underestimated. Knowing that you've got someone coming over will give you a lift and help you get through the day.

You'll get a similar lift from seeing your friends who have children. Of course it's not realistic to expect them to offer any practical help, although many will try, but it's often the case that your toddler will behave better and your baby will feed better if there are other people around, simply because you are happier and more relaxed. So invite them over, feed them, deal with even more mess and chaos, then – the best bit – you'll hopefully get invited back. And visiting other people is a great way of coping in the early days – your toddler will be entertained and fed and you'll have an opportunity to feed your baby.

Breastfeeding

The first 6 weeks of breastfeeding are full of challenges, but if you can get through this period you will almost certainly be able to continue breastfeeding your baby long term.

The first month will be particularly tough if you are breastfeeding, because new babies drink so slowly. But things will become easier over the next few weeks. By about week 4 your baby will take around 40 minutes to feed, rather than an hour, and also be able to last longer between feeds, up to 4 hours on occasion. And by week 6 she will need fewer feeds a day – between 6 and 10 over 24 hours.

Do watch out for growth spurts at around weeks 3 and 6, when your baby will have an insatiable appetite and want constant feeding for a couple of days. When you've got another child it is especially hard to find enough time to feed your baby, so prepare for the growth spurts by piling up DVDs and toys ready to keep your toddler amused, and even getting a bit of help if possible. Then feed and feed your baby, knowing that this phase will pass in a couple of days. The end-result of constant demand feeding is that you produce more milk, which will of course make things easier once the growth spurt is over.

Another challenge of breastfeeding when you've got an older child is resisting the temptation to rush the end of a feed, or being too quick to swap your baby to your other breast. If you do this she will go short of the rich, fatty hindmilk. This helps babies last longer between feeds. So allow your baby to get into the slow-sucking, dopey, end-of-feed-state, which happens after about 25 minutes.

A Word to Dads

As you know from previously, having a new baby makes life incredibly busy. This time your partner will be more desperate than ever for you to muck in and help with the childcare, even though you're also expected to get up and go to work after yet another broken night.

And when you get home your partner may well be exhausted, bad-tempered and unlikely to want to listen to your work problems, let alone hear about any office news.

The early weeks of having a second baby are certainly no honeymoon, but in a few weeks from now, things will start to settle as the baby becomes easier to look after. In the meantime, here are some strategies to get you through.

First, it goes without saying that you need to do as much as you can to help in the early weeks, especially with your older child, as this will free up your partner to care for the baby. But if you're working all hours, then give your partner a promise of childcare to look forward to. For example, tell her that you'll take the children out for 2 hours on Saturday morning. And do it. Or perhaps you could promise to come home early on Friday and bath the toddler and sort out dinner (a takeaway or a ready meal counts). By making your partner a promise and sticking to it, you'll not only be giving her practical help, but also something to look forward to – which will seem like a lifeline in the middle of the week when she's struggling on her own with both children.

Secondly, tell your partner that she's doing well and you don't know how she copes. Better still, *ask* how she copes. If she'd just run a marathon you'd be full of admiration and want to hear the details of how she'd succeeded. Well, she's quite likely to be feeling as though she has run a marathon and would love to talk through how she did it. It may sound trivial that she managed to get the baby and toddler down for an afternoon nap at the same time, but for your partner this is a ground-breaking step forward and is potentially life-changing because it gives her time to herself during the day.

BABY 🔊

The biggest challenge around now is breastfeeding your baby, as we've already said. But do note that even bottle-fed babies will demand milk around the clock, and take their time drinking it. But just as with breastfed babies, although it's tough now it will soon become much easier.

On the subject of bottles, if your baby is breastfed then it's worth giving her an occasional bottle by about week 3 to ensure that she becomes used to it and doesn't reject bottles later on when you may wish to express or leave her with someone else.

Bottle-feeding can be a lovely activity for your older child to help with – if he wants to, of course. As a rough guide to how much your toddler can 'help' feed his baby sibling, a 2½-year-old can hold the bottle while you hold the baby, and a child of 7 will be able to hold the baby and bottle by himself – although don't leave the room in case the baby chokes or your older child becomes bored.

Another reason newborns are so challenging is that they poo so often. We said in the last chapter that your baby may well be pooing after every feed. Do console yourself that the constant nappy-changing will improve – by 6 weeks babies do up to 6 poos a day (hopefully less), so there'll be far fewer nappies to change. Likewise your baby will be weeing less frequently.

And finally, colic can start from about 3 to 4 weeks. This is stressful enough when you have just one baby, but when you've got another child you'll really have your hands full. On the upside, you'll be more relaxed as a second-time mum and less flustered by the crying. This in itself will help calm your baby. You can also use props – a baby sling, a dummy, or colic drops. None of these is miraculous, but combined they may help a little. And, as we've mentioned, don't rush feeds if you are breastfeeding, because drinking lots of foremilk (and not enough hindmilk) can make wind worse for babies.

Even if your baby doesn't have colic, you'll notice that as she drinks faster she'll take in more air and need winding – sometimes she won't burp until 40 minutes after her feed.

As if these early weeks weren't difficult enough – there's a general pattern for newborns to cry more and more each week until they peak at 6 weeks, when some babies may cry for several hours a day. Thankfully, after this period crying gradually reduces. Also, lots of mums find that their second and subsequent babies cry far less than their first – quite possibly because they are more skilled in feeding and winding, and also a lot more relaxed.

The main reason your baby will cry in the early weeks is hunger. Thankfully she won't cry yet from tiredness. This is one of the blessings in the first 6 weeks – when a new baby feels tired she'll simply fall asleep and is unlikely to become overtired. She may also cry if she has wind, but she'll fall asleep as soon as she has expelled any trapped air.

Try to give your baby some time on her tummy – this is even better for muscle development than being flat on her back, and will help to build her upper back and neck muscles. You can put your baby on her tummy from around 2 weeks. Although at first she'll only be happy for a couple of minutes, persevere and she'll gradually build up her tummy time, as well as her muscles. Your older child can encourage his sibling to stay on her tummy for longer by lying down opposite her and pulling faces. Don't put your baby down to sleep on her tummy, though, because of the risk of cot death.

When it comes to bathing your baby, you can quickly wash her in the bath while your toddler is bathing, then get her dry and changed on the bathroom floor (on a changing mat) while your toddler continues to play in the bath. As we said in the last chapter, you need to be organized and have everything to hand so that you don't leave your toddler alone in the bathroom.

··

TIPS FOR ESTABLISHING A ROUTINE

You can start preparing your baby for a routine by getting her into the habit of falling asleep on her own – so put her into her Moses basket when she seems dozy rather than letting her always fall asleep in your arms or while she's feeding. There's no need to be too regimented – it's actually rather lovely having your baby fall asleep in your arms, and for many mums this may be your last baby, so enjoy her. Just ensure that she falls asleep by herself a couple of times a day.

··

TODDLER ⒶⒷⒸ

Jealousy may occur around now, if it hasn't already – the novelty of having a new baby has worn off and it will dawn on your toddler that the baby is still here and is going to stay.

Signs of jealousy are many and varied – hitting the baby, regressive behaviour, more tantrums and general 'naughtiness' are all signs that your toddler resents the baby.

Try not to take much notice of any poor behaviour – telling your toddler off gives him attention, even if it is negative. And if you get really angry he'll start to hate his sibling and feel very unloved as he watches you gently cuddle and feed her.

A more effective way to manage his behaviour is to give him positive attention. Cuddle and play with him as often as you can (more on one-to-one on page 81). And give your toddler plenty of praise. You may have to scrape a bit if he's really misbehaving, but even something simple like holding onto the buggy nicely can be praised. Giving praise has instant results, because it not only rewards good behaviour but also alters the way you speak to your toddler, so breaking a cycle of you telling him off constantly and him winding you up to get attention. Try to give descriptive praise where you comment on specific behaviour – 'You did really well tidying up your toys' – rather than bland praise where you say things like 'good boy'.

Your toddler's need for attention is usually the root cause of any change in behaviour – he thinks you're giving the baby more attention than him, and will do what he can to change this.

This explains why it's common for toddlers to regress when a new baby arrives. So he may want to start drinking from a bottle again, or perhaps wear a nappy (even if he's toilet-trained). Regression is a classic reaction that toddlers have when their baby sibling is born. If you play along, perhaps saying that there are twin babies now who both need looking after, this phase is unlikely to go on for more than a few weeks, and may well be over in a matter of days. So find your toddler a baby bottle, or put a nappy on over his clothes (hopefully he'll be happy with this and won't want to actually use a nappy). It's also important to emphasize how grown-up your toddler is – he'll hopefully enjoy getting attention for being a big boy more than for drinking out of a baby bottle.

Of course it's not easy to give your toddler attention when you're trying to feed, change and wind your baby. We covered toddler entertainment during breastfeeding in Chapter 5, and here we cover winding and nappy-changing.

Winding

It can be difficult winding a baby with your toddler running about, especially if your baby is having painful, colic-like spasms. Try making winding into a game. Your toddler will be highly amused when his baby sibling does a big burp, and may want to co-operate with rubbing her back.

Another way for a toddler to help wind a colicky baby is for him to sit on the sofa, right at the back so that he is stable and his back is well supported, then you can place the baby tummy-down across your toddler's knees, so that he can rub her back. Take care that your baby's face doesn't get squashed into the sofa and that she can breathe. Reassure your toddler if she cries and explain that being on her front helps her tummy-ache. If he doesn't want to hold the baby, or becomes bored, you can always suggest that he winds his favourite toy.

Once your toddler understands about winding, you'll find that he's reassured by the fact that you're not just cuddling and rubbing your baby's back for the sake of it, and as a result he'll be more patient.

Nappy-changing

Just as your toddler may have fun 'breastfeeding' his favourite toy, he may also enjoy changing its nappy. Give him a couple of nappies and even an empty pot of nappy cream to play with while you change your baby's nappy. You can still use any nappies your toddler has played with later.

If you ever have to abandon your baby during a nappy change to attend to your toddler, you can pick up the changing mat with her still on it and place it on the floor. Doing this means that regardless of what stage of the nappy change you have reached, you can still rush to your toddler.

CHILD 👶

It's quite common for children to say that they hate their new baby. Your immediate reaction will probably be to tell them that they can't say that. However, it's actually very important that your child is allowed to say he hates the baby, and a much better reaction from you would be, 'Yes, it is hard having a new baby around – they need lots of feeding and nappy-changing and make Mummy and Daddy very tired.'

By saying this you're not agreeing with your child, but you are allowing him to voice his feelings and acknowledge his anger. This is a major life event and your child is entitled to have strong feelings about it. He's used to being the little one and an only child, and this is a big thing to get used to.

If you don't allow your child to express his anger, he'll have to bottle it up and it will probably re-emerge as behavioural problems. It's not unusual for small children to vent their anger on Mum – hitting and kicking her, or clinging to Dad while glaring at Mum. There's little point in focusing on the hating-Mum behaviour (he still loves you very much but feels extremely hurt). Responding harshly would make him feel even more hurt and insecure. It's far better to find a quiet moment and ask simply, 'Are you feeling cross with me because I've had another baby?' Helping your child to voice his feelings will be reassuring and calming for him.

Try to accept that it's actually quite normal to find a new baby irritating – after all, she cries a lot, then just as you're all about to go out she poos and delays things, the constant feeding is boring, and you're too tired and tied up to do as much as previously. There are things you can do to help your child through these tedious times:

1. Just as you find it reassuring to know that the crying, feeding and pooing will improve, your child will, too. So take the time to explain to him the improvements he can expect. And don't blame the baby for not being able to do fun things, for example if you say, 'We can't go to the park this afternoon because the baby needs feeding,' this will result in resentment. We all do this without thinking, but try instead to say, 'Once I've fed the baby we can do some drawing,' and so on.

2. Make the tedium into a game – perhaps keep a 'poo chart' for how many dirty nappies the baby does a day.

3. Collude, as we've said before. So lots of shared eye-rolling when the baby starts crying.

4. Try to play with your child. Just once a day for 15 minutes will have a noticeable effect. But any amount of one-to-one time will benefit him. Talking intimately doesn't count – children will talk about their feelings in their own time, not when you decide. Instead, play with him, for example a board game or a puzzle. Your child will find this time therapeutic and relaxing – all he wants is to play with Mummy and to know that he's not forgotten. And he may sometimes talk about

PROTEST POOING

Occasionally a young child will react to a new baby by deliberately pooing in his pants or weeing all over the floor to get attention (this often happens when you are breastfeeding because all your attention will be on the baby and not your child). The result of such a protest is instant attention from you and, as far as your child is concerned, it is mission accomplished because he's the centre of attention and the new baby is being ignored and even abandoned mid-feed.

Should your child make such a protest, the worst thing you can do is to get cross – very difficult as you'll probably be feeling furious. But this would actually fuel his behaviour because he's feeling deeply angry about the new baby and is desperate for your attention and will actually get some satisfaction from making you angry, too. Instead, stay calm and clean up as quickly as possible to minimize the fuss and attention you give to your toddler. Once you're settled again with the baby, give your eldest some positive attention, perhaps telling him a story.

You can expect a repeat performance at the next feed, but if you minimize your response he'll probably stop after about a week or two. And it can sometime help to talk to your child about how he's feeling about the new baby – on his terms, of course. So if he brings up the subject of the baby, help him to verbalize his feelings – he'll be less angry and so less likely to protest.

Children still in nappies may put their hands down inside their dirty nappy and smear poo all over the place. Again, respond with a minimum of fuss. And also, dress your child in clothes that stop him reaching his nappy – dungarees work well.

the baby during these times together. Don't play electronic or computer games during your precious time together, as these are too absorbing and don't allow you to communicate.

HOUSEKEEPING

If you have no childcare during the week, then use weekends to catch up as your partner will hopefully be around. So cook batches of food to freeze, have a nap, tidy up, do your shopping (even online shopping needs an uninterrupted hour) – anything that will make your forthcoming week a little easier.

Don't become too obsessed with domestic order or you'll end up exhausted and also demoralized, as the chaos will inevitably return very quickly. It's actually more important at this stage to spend time as a family – not easy in the early days but you'll all feel better for making the effort to go out, even if it's just to a local park.

If you need some space but your partner is reluctant to take both children (quite likely if you are breastfeeding and your baby seems to still be feeding constantly), then split the family in half. Your partner and eldest child can spend time together while you take your baby out on your own, perhaps to see a friend – this will seem like a break as it's much easier to have a coffee and a chat while looking after a baby than while chasing around after a toddler. Already you'll find looking after just one child at a time a doddle compared with looking after two.

Book a cleaner for Monday mornings if you can afford or justify it, because that way you won't spend time worrying about the ever-mounting chaos during the weekend but will feel more inclined to play and have fun with your family, or just catch up on some much-needed sleep.

If you have childcare during the week, or your eldest is at school or nursery, then weekends may actually feel more like a challenge than a break. The big advantage is that you will look forward to Monday mornings when you can have a rest – you'll find that looking forward to this will help to keep you going when things kick off.

Registering Your Baby, Applying for Child Benefit, Booking Your 6-week Check

There's quite a lot of admin to do when you have a baby. You'll need to book your 6-week check for you and your baby, and you can take your toddler's red book along so that he can get weighed and measured and not feel too left out.

You'll also need to get your baby registered. If you're married, then either you or your husband can do this, with the baby of course – you don't all have to go. And don't forget to apply for Child Benefit – you get slightly less money for subsequent children than for your first. This can be backdated by up to 3 months, but beyond this you will lose money. You'll need to send your child's birth certificate and an application form to the Inland Revenue.

TROUBLESHOOTING

Who do I go to first when both my children are crying?

One of the biggest challenges of being a parent is when both children are crying. This can seem pretty overwhelming, but thankfully it never lasts long.

Sometimes it's obvious who to go to first, for example if one of them is in danger. But often this happens because the baby needs feeding, is overtired or has wind, and your toddler is either hungry, has hurt himself or is frustrated – usually over something quite minor such not being able to fit some railway track together. If no one's in danger we suggest attending your toddler first – he'll appreciate you prioritizing him, whereas your baby will be unaware that she is 'second'. Tend to your toddler quickly and don't let him drag out his recovery time, leaving the baby to cry excessively. Once you've given your toddler something to eat, stuck a plaster on him or fixed a toy, you'll need to sort your baby out even if your toddler is still crying. Do reassure your toddler, and resist getting cross if he's still crying (quite challenging, as you'll be feeling stressed). Explain that you've helped him and now you must help the baby, too – eventually he'll learn to share your time.

As your baby gets older, there will be times when it is appropriate to help her first. More on this in Chapter 8.

In the meantime, here's a helpful trick to help you cope with the stress of when both your children are crying. Set a kitchen timer for 1 minute and we can pretty much guarantee that the situation will improve slightly in this time, and you'll almost certainly have calmed one of your children down within 3 minutes. Staying calm when your toddler is throwing a tantrum and your baby is purple with hunger-rage is something that comes with experience. However, when you're new to this it's easy to become very wound up – that's why the kitchen timer trick can work, as it demonstrates how quickly these situations pass. After a while you'll actually find the action of setting the timer soothing in itself, because it will give you a sense of control in a pretty out-of-control situation.

Sometimes I feel too tired to get everyone ready in the morning – is it OK to stay at home all day and skip playgroup?

We do suggest in our daily plan that you have a busy morning with your toddler and a relaxing afternoon. This seems to work for most mums, because however much effort it takes to get everyone out, the alternative can be worse because your toddler can become bored and have a surplus of energy, then find it difficult to settle later in the day. However, if your toddler isn't particularly energetic or you have a garden, you may get away with spending entire days at home, which can be very pleasant in these early weeks. You'll still need to keep your toddler entertained, but as you do nice things together, cooking for example, he'll come to love being at home. If you want him to enjoy the garden, go outside and enjoy it yourself. Your baby can even nap outside in her pram while you and your toddler kick a ball to wear him out. It's fine for your baby to sleep outside in her pram in winter, as long as she is wrapped up. After all, it's no different from pushing her to the shops. You'll no doubt find that your baby sleeps better in the garden, and you and your toddler feel calmer, too. It won't be long before your toddler is happy to play by himself in the garden, because he'll associate it with having a lovely time with Mum.

My partner doesn't seem interested in the baby but spends all his time with our eldest

It's very often the case that Mum looks after the new baby and Dad looks after the eldest child. But this can leave you feeling really anxious that the father–baby bond isn't happening because your partner doesn't seem particularly interested in the baby, especially compared with your first-born. This is very common and nothing to worry about – the father–baby bond nearly always develops, even if it takes a few weeks or even months. In the meantime, Dad can develop a lovely, strong bond with his eldest child.

There's always the option of swapping roles. Doing this may encourage the father–baby bond, especially once the baby is smiling by 6 weeks. But it will also give you a chance to spend time with your eldest on his own – he'll appreciate having you to himself rather than having to share you with the baby.

CHAPTER 7
The Early Weeks: 6–12

From around 6 weeks, life begins to get slightly easier as your baby becomes gradually less demanding and you start to get more used to looking after two children. You can even begin nudging your baby into a routine – although nothing too regimented at this stage. But you will notice the beginnings of a feeding and sleeping pattern emerging over the next few weeks, and we'll explain how to encourage this. This will certainly make your days a little smoother, but realistically it's unlikely that you will get your baby into a really predictable routine until she is over 3 months old.

But the big thing that's going to happen from around 6 weeks is that your baby will become aware of her surroundings, interested in who she sees, and will start smiling. This is not only exciting for you but for your eldest child, too. Up until now he's probably found his baby sibling a little dull – at the very most she may have given him a wide-eyed, surprised stare. But this will change once the baby starts not only to notice her elder sibling as he goes about his day-to-day life, but to react to him. It's wonderful to watch your children as they begin to interact and, with a little guidance, they can start to 'play' together.

It's interesting to note that babies have the capacity to become bored from around 6 weeks. But this is rarely an issue for second babies because they have an older sibling to watch – even a temper tantrum is wonderful entertainment for a baby.

MUM

Babies at around this age seem to lose that almost weightless quality of newborns. So even though your baby seems incredibly light compared with your older child, you may start to become physically more tired as she gets bigger – after all, you'll be forever lifting and carrying her at this age – up and down stairs, picking her up when she cries and so on. If you're also lifting a toddler, this will put even more physical demands on you. Likewise, if you're using a double buggy this will become harder to push as your children grow.

Here are a couple of things that will help. First, as your children grow so will your muscles. And secondly, use a baby carrier to carry your baby around your home – it's easier than carrying her in your arms. We've suggested this in previous chapters, and if you haven't got yourself sorted with a sling yet, it's certainly not too late – children can be in these up until the age of about 4 years. And if your baby seems too heavy to carry in her sling, then change it – as we've said previously, we particularly recommend an Ergo carrier, which lots of mums say is the most comfortable.

But even if you've got strong muscles and a good carrier, it will still be tiring carrying a heavy load for much of the day, so do allow for this and don't try to get too much other stuff done.

On the upside, it will help to get you fit and burn more calories. It's generally harder to get back into shape after your second baby than your first because a lot of the time you will be dawdling along slowly rather than being able to power walk with the buggy. You've also got the added temptation of picking at your toddler's food, which doesn't help matters. It's probably unrealistic to even think about exercising while your baby is under 3 months and you're coping with another child too. So we don't return to that subject until Chapter 9.

For now, a weekly Pilates class can be a great way to start exercising, as this not only works your pelvic floor muscles, but it is also an almost guaranteed hour a week to relax and de-stress.

During these stressful early weeks, some mums find themselves secretly favouring one child over the other. It's quite likely to be your baby, as she will seem more vulnerable, whereas your older child will probably have attitude and tantrums. On the other hand, if your baby is colicky and particularly demanding you may resent the constant attention that she requires and long to have some fun with your older child.

We cover favourites in more detail in Chapter 12, but in the meantime it can be useful to seek the company of close friends or relatives who particularly adore your 'least favoured' child. So if Grandma has gone gooey-eyed over the new baby, spend time watching them together and seeing your baby through Grandma's adoring eyes. Likewise, if your partner thinks your eldest can do no wrong, watch them playing and laughing together and any feelings of criticism will soon soften.

Breastfeeding

This usually settles by now and your breasts will be softer and won't leak as much now that your milk has adjusted to your baby's demands. This makes breastfeeding easier when you are out because your baby will be able to latch on very quickly. Also problems with sore nipples and mastitis are far less likely now. So you've reached the stage where it is possible, although not necessarily desirable, to walk across a room to sort your toddler out while still breastfeeding.

Do be aware that babies have another growth spurt at about 6 weeks. So, once again, you'll be feeding around the clock for a couple of days. And from 10 weeks your baby will be more distracted during feeds and may well want to watch your toddler instead of feeding. This is because her eyesight has developed and she can see across the room. There are two options here – put a cloth loosely over her head so that she can't see what's going on, or encourage your toddler to be less 'entertaining', perhaps by reading a book together while your baby feeds.

When your baby seems distracted, take care that this doesn't mark the beginning of a habit developing when your baby feeds less and less during the day, then makes up for it at night. More on this in Chapter 8.

BABY

From now your baby will start to smile, so do take time to enjoy this delightful stage. Very often these early tentative, fleeting smiles will be at an older sibling who will no doubt smile back, encouraging the baby to smile again. This can be very touching and a good opportunity for you to spell out how much the baby loves her older brother or sister.

At 6 weeks your baby's crying will peak and she'll go through another growth spurt, but from then on her crying will start to recede and she'll suffer less and less from wind or colic until this pretty much disappears by 3 months. In the meantime, go out as much as you can – the movement of the buggy or being in a sling will help to soothe your baby. And your eldest will appreciate not being stuck at home with a crying baby and a very stressed mother.

Another thing that happens at 6 weeks, as we've said previously, is that your baby will become a little harder to settle as she starts to fight sleep – meaning that she can become over-tired. So you can start to think about a daytime napping routine that will help you distinguish between hunger and tiredness – your baby will often ask to be fed when she's actually tired.

TIPS FOR ESTABLISHING A ROUTINE

Ideally, babies have 3 naps a day, totalling at least 3 hours if possible. The first nap lasts about 30 to 40 minutes, about 2 hours after she wakes in the morning. This may coincide with you walking or driving to school, nursery or playgroup. Or perhaps your baby will drop off to sleep while you're getting ready in the morning. If this happens, just ensure that she's well fed before you set off – babies can go for around 3 hours from the start of one feed to the start of another. So if you start her first feed at around 7 a.m., she'll need her next one at about 10 a.m.

The lunchtime nap is the longest of the day and will eventually last a couple of hours, and perhaps correlate with your toddler's nap or quiet time. And finally, your baby will need a late afternoon nap, for about 30 to 40 minutes.

At this stage you should only regard this as a rough guide to napping and not attempt to follow it too closely or you'll end up frustrated – you're far more likely to get your baby into this napping pattern between 3 and 6 months. But if you know what you are eventually aiming for, you'll be able to nudge your baby into a napping pattern that fits in with the family timetable, perhaps coordinating her naps with your toddler's afternoon sleep or when you're preparing tea.

TODDLER Ⓐ Ⓑ Ⓒ

You'll discover over the next few months and years that whenever your baby passes a milestone, your toddler (or older child, for that matter) can become jealous. It's not the milestone itself that causes problems, but how parents react – you're suddenly giving the baby excessive amounts of praise and attention, and this riles your eldest child.

Smiling is certainly one of these milestones. And if your toddler starts playing up or regressing, chances are it's because he's watched you delight in your baby's first tentative smiles as your gaze at her, grinning for all you're worth.

You obviously can't ignore your baby's milestones – your affection and praise are essential for her development. But you can involve your toddler so that he doesn't feel excluded. Tell him that the baby is learning to smile and because he is so grown-up he can help to teach her. And make sure you admire his lovely big smile and clean white teeth – anything to reassure and praise him. Do assure your toddler that the baby really likes him – this is very easy to do once the baby starts smiling at him, as we've previously mentioned.

Play is extremely important to children. But finding time to play with your toddler can seem impossible when you're exhausted and already pushed to your limits. We suggest you set a timer, even for just 5 minutes. Knowing that you'll be able to get back to your tasks and baby after this tiny amount of time will stop you from putting off play until later.

If you can manage a short play session every day, you'll soon find that your toddler is better behaved and that play actually becomes a time-saver because you won't waste so much time sorting out tantrums.

We said in the last chapter how some toddlers love to look after a favourite soft toy as though it were a baby. If your toddler is still enjoying this, you could buy some kit for his 'baby' such as a buggy, a feeding bottle (although he may choose to 'breastfeed') and later on, a high chair.

During bathtime you can encourage your toddler to have fun with the baby, who is now old enough to really enjoy her baths and respond to her sibling. Put your baby in a bath chair to free your hands, then show your toddler how to pour water over the baby's tummy. He'll probably want to pat the baby's tummy, as it will be lovely and round. And your baby is old enough to start kicking quite vigorously, so your toddler can use the 'current' to move a small plastic boat or other floating toy. If he's not interested in the baby, don't push it. And if he suddenly becomes irritated and splashes the baby, don't make too much of a big deal about it, just take the baby out of the bath.

At this stage we'd still recommend that your toddler has a longer bath and you pop the baby in and out, getting her ready on the bathroom floor (on a changing mat). Over the coming months your baby will enjoy spending gradually longer playing in the bath. By the time she's a year old she'll be having a lovely time playing with her older sibling, perhaps even getting out after him (see Chapter 10).

CHILD

Just as toddlers can struggle with baby milestones, older children can, too. So each time your baby passes a milestone, it's important to lavish plenty of attention on your older child.

When it comes to bathtime, it's generally easier to get everyone ready for bed together. But until the baby is about 10 months there's a small risk that the baby may poo in the bath, which an older child would find disgusting. So we suggest that you take everyone up to the bathroom together, but bath your baby and child separately.

Avoiding Homework Battles

If your child has homework this can be quite challenging to supervise when you've got a baby. It's important that your child doesn't think he can get away with not doing his homework now that the baby is born. So here are some strategies to help:

1. Tell the school about your newborn and explain that your child is now struggling with homework. If you've got the school's support, you'll relax and this will instantly make it easier to calmly insist your child does his homework – he's far more likely to respond to this than to an over-emotional homework battle.

2.   Set up a reward chart for a couple of weeks to help things along.

3.   Give lots of descriptive praise, for example: 'Your handwriting is so neat these days,' 'You're reading fluently, a bit like an adult,' 'Gosh, you worked that sum out quickly,' and so on.

4.   Try doing reading homework in bed in the morning – lots of mums with young babies find this works, because your child will be getting more obvious attention than his feeding sibling.

5.   Wait until the weekend, when you'll hopefully have more help and so uninterrupted time to both help your child with homework and also to insist he does it in the first place.

6.   Try an after-school homework club – but ensure your child is happy with this. He shouldn't feel pushed out of the home as a punishment.

7.   Use the tried-and-tested method of no TV or computer games until homework is done. This nearly always works, even if it takes a week of your child 'happily' playing with toys instead of watching television before he caves in.

HOUSEKEEPING

Now that your baby is smiling and gurgling it becomes more difficult to use the excuse of having a newborn baby to justify takeaway meals and domestic chaos. But the reality is that you will be busier than ever and still won't have the time or energy for much housekeeping at the moment. So you can either pay someone else to help or, if this isn't an option, cheat. Here are some domestic shortcuts you can take:

Laundry

To reduce the volume of washing, use bibs for your baby and toddler; sponge clothes clean at the end of a meal; avoid white clothes; don't wash anything unless it is noticeably dirty or smelly; and change bed linen less often (this is only for the first couple of months!).

Instead of ironing, you can shake your wet washing really hard and hang it very neatly to dry – this works well for cotton t-shirts and trousers, but isn't so effective for viscose, silk, or tops with collars.

Cooking

Buy prepared ingredients such as grated cheese, ready-chopped onions, tubes of garlic paste, ready-washed and chopped vegetables and salads, and prepared fruit such as pineapples and melons. It may be more expensive to shop this way, and also less healthy than eating freshly chopped fruit and vegetables, but in the early weeks you'll be grateful not to have to do these tasks, as they take time and also two hands – you'll find yourself doing an awful lot one-handed at this stage. Frozen vegetables are also useful as they are both ready-prepared and cheaper than fresh.

You can also buy ready-prepared gingerbread mix from supermarkets, as well as cookie and bread dough. This is an easy way to do some baking with your eldest when you're feeling exhausted.

Don't underestimate ready meals, which can save you a lot of time. For example, it probably takes at least an hour to make a lasagne by the time you've cleared up, so why not buy one? Admittedly it will probably be higher in fat and salt and also more expensive (although frozen is cheaper than fresh). And of course it won't taste as good. But in these tough early weeks, it's probably worth considering.

If you do cook, then cook in bulk and freeze some. And don't try new recipes in the early weeks, as they take up too much mental energy. Also your eldest may refuse to eat new food and be very fussy, which you'll find difficult to cope with if you've gone to the effort of trying a new recipe, not to mention the fact that you are tired.

Cleaning

Clear floors, as this is nearly as effective as vacuuming. Using a dustpan and brush under your toddler's high chair is quicker than sweeping the entire floor. Visitors notice clutter more than dust – so shove things into cupboards. They will also notice dirt on things they come into contact with, so wipe the table if it is sticky and clean the sink and toilet. It doesn't have to be thorough – a quick rub with a couple of baby wipes can do the trick. And a squirt of blue toilet cleaner down the loo creates a good impression and takes 10 seconds.

TROUBLESHOOTING

I find car trips a nightmare because it's so hard to get both my children and the buggy in and out of the car

As a general rule, your older child should be first in and last out of the car. Once he's strapped in you'll have time to put your baby in and also load up the buggy and anything else you may need without the worry of your toddler escaping. Likewise, when you arrive get the buggy out first, put the baby in (or put her into a baby carrier), then get your toddler out last, by which time you will be organized and able to stop him from running across a road or car park.

If, in an emergency, you need your toddler to wait, tell him to keep two hands on the side of the car, a nearby wall or anywhere else he will be safe. This is more effective than simply telling him to wait, which he probably won't be able to do. He will, however, be able to place his hands on a wall, hopefully for up to about 10 seconds – more on a good day.

Car journeys can be extremely stressful with young children, and when you have two children this stress can escalate exponentially if both children are crying. Long journeys are obviously more problematic than short ones, so always ensure that your children aren't too hot, hungry or thirsty. You can cut the stress altogether by travelling at night if possible – if you set off just before bedtime, your children will hopefully sleep for the entire journey.

I take my toddler out each morning but he still gets restless again later

Some toddlers are particularly energetic and need to be taken out twice a day – just as big dogs need two walks a day to keep them happy. If this is the case with your child, although it's tedious getting everyone ready to go out again in the afternoon, on balance this is less stressful than staying in. It doesn't have to be a long or elaborate trip – going to a local shop, a park or even to see some nearby roadworks (fascinating for young children) should do the trick. Just ensure that your toddler walks, or has a chance to run, so that he gets some exercise.

If you go out at the same time each day, this can be a good opportunity for your baby to have her late afternoon nap. Time your return for about half an hour before tea and your baby will hopefully continue to sleep on your return, allowing you to prepare the meal. Then your baby should wake for a feed while your toddler eats tea. The reality may of course be different, but if you persist with this routine your baby will gradually fit into this pattern – just ensure she is well fed before you go for your afternoon walk.

CHAPTER 8
Months 3–6

Your baby is now old enough to fall into a feeding and sleeping pattern and will also become willing to have 'early nights'. So you can aim at getting both children off to sleep by around 7 p.m. and having your evenings back (that's assuming your eldest is 5 or younger). This is a real sanity-saver because, whatever is going on during the day, you'll be able to say to yourself that you only have to keep going until 7 p.m., by which time both children will be in bed.

It can sometimes take longer to get a routine established with your second baby. This is because you'll be more relaxed and blasé about the chaos of a new baby – so rather than clock-watching and carefully planning her routines, you'll be far more likely to take the easy option and cuddle your baby non-stop and continue to feed her on demand.

Also, night-feeds won't seem nearly as traumatic as with your first baby because you know it soon ends – again, this will mean that you won't be as desperate to get your baby into a routine as previously. Add this to the fact that you'll be more tired looking after two children (especially with a close age gap), and it's a miracle that second babies ever get into a routine at all!

Having said that, if your eldest is at nursery or school, you'll have a daily structure forced upon you and may well find that your baby is already in some sort of routine, however haphazard. Plenty of mothers say that their second baby fell into a routine sooner because day-to-day life was more structured.

But whatever your circumstances, 3 months is the ideal age to get your baby into a routine, as she's old enough to be able to go at least 3 hours between feeds, and to sleep for at least 5 hours non-stop. But she's still young enough not to be too resistant to a change of habit. In this chapter we give a step-by-step guide to establishing a routine (see the Baby section on pages 104–105).

✚ IMMUNIZATIONS ✚

Your baby's immunizations will be due at around 12 weeks and again at 16 weeks, assuming she had her first lot at 8 weeks.

MUM

If you've ever found yourself breastfeeding the baby while bathing your eldest and asking yourself, 'When's this nightmare going to end?' you're certainly not alone. But as your baby gets older and you settle her into a routine you'll hopefully start to feel human again. It's possible to see an improvement within days.

Do be aware that postnatal depression can start at around 4 months. Even if you didn't suffer with your first baby, it doesn't rule out you suffering with subsequent children. So look out for signs, including sustained feelings of helplessness or hopelessness, sleeplessness, withdrawal from friends and family, and a loss of appetite.

A report by the charity 4Children has found that up to 3 in 10 mothers suffer, but sadly many suffer in silence because they are too embarrassed to admit being depressed, as this would make them feel like a failure as a mother. Mums also worry that Social Services will intervene and take their children away if social workers find out they have postnatal depression. This wouldn't happen. What would happen is that you'd probably be offered around six counselling sessions, which many mothers find extremely helpful for getting through the early months, and possibly anti-depressants may also be prescribed. But most importantly, you would be offered support and sympathy from your health visitor and GP, who are very used to dealing with postnatal depression.

If you're not sure whether you're depressed or just exhausted, simply visit your GP. Whether or not your doctor thinks you're depressed, he or she will offer kindness which, let's face it, all mums of young children need.

You can also take an online test at www.testandcalc.com/etc/tests/edin.asp. This is a link for the Edinburgh Postnatal Depression Scale, which has 10 questions used by doctors to identify women who may be suffering from postnatal depression. Do talk to your health visitor or GP if your score is 10 or above.

For more information on postnatal depression you can visit www.mind.org.

Breastfeeding

Your baby will have another growth spurt at around 3 months, but this won't take over your life in quite the same way as previously because she won't be feeding as often these days – she'll be having 5 to 8 feeds a day, a couple fewer than previously. But, as with other growth spurts, do prepare so that you can put the extra time into feeding your baby. And if you've managed to establish any sort of routine or order, be prepared for this to be obliterated for a couple of days.

Your baby will be able to cope a little better these days if you feed her slightly late – this is quite likely to happen if you are going out more. Although this makes life easier, take care that you don't relax *too* much. It's easy to end up in a situation where your baby doesn't get enough milk during the day, then wants to make up for it at night. The problem is that now your baby is bigger, she'll be able to go for much of the day without feeding if she's had a lot of milk at night. Then a cycle begins: you become more tired from night-feeding and looking after two children, so you pop your baby into your bed at night to feed.

It's a tough pattern to break. So do ensure that your baby feeds well during the day so that she doesn't become a night-only feeder. If this does happen, you can break the cycle by not feeding your baby after 4 a.m., but allowing her to feed at 7 a.m. or later – her first daytime feed. You'll probably have to be awake, rocking and soothing her for some of this time, as she'll be used to being fed, and it will be exhausting. But if you can hold out until 7 a.m. your baby will have a big feed and you'll be well on the way to breaking the night-feeding pattern.

BABY

Your baby will start laughing at around 3 months, and will become increasingly fascinated by her surroundings, particularly her elder sibling. This is when their relationship really starts to get established, and you'll see that the more your eldest laughs, the more your baby will smile and laugh in response.

Your baby may start rolling from 5 months, and some babies even start crawling by 6 months. Be sure to give her plenty of tummy time – not easy when you've got another child, but essential for your baby's muscle development.

Also from 5 months, your baby can sit up in the buggy. So if she's sharing a double buggy she could swap places with her sibling – we suggest you let your eldest decide on the seating arrangements, as your baby is still too young to care. But plenty of toddlers will enjoy the cosseting experience of riding in the 'baby' seat.

A few babies will sleep for 12 hours uninterrupted by the time they are 6 months, although it's more realistic to aim for 5 hours uninterrupted at night. And from 3 months your baby will have pretty much stopped pooing at night and weeing when you change her.

TIPS FOR ESTABLISHING A ROUTINE

If you don't have any sort of routine yet but want one, begin by sorting out feeding patterns. We talked about your baby's daytime napping pattern in the last chapter in the hope that it would help you to distinguish between hunger and tiredness. But now that your baby is older you can work hard on her feeding pattern because she can go longer between feeds. Having big, satisfying regular feeds will further help her sleeping pattern.

So aim to feed her only every 3 hours. Your baby will be upset if she's used to more, but distract her, hold her and try to get her to wait. The first time will be the hardest, but then she'll have a huge feed and it will be easier after that.

Once your baby is feeding every 3 hours or longer, and has dropped any snacking habits, you can focus on her sleep. We described a napping timetable in the last chapter. To help get this established you can cheat! So rock her, sing, put her in the buggy. You're aiming to teach your baby to feel tired at these times. After a couple of days you'll notice that she does indeed start to become tired at these times. When this happens you can put her in her cot and gradually reduce how much help you give her to get to sleep. Once she can settle herself in the day, she'll be able to do the same during the night.

Going on holiday around now is relatively easy, as your baby isn't yet mobile – certainly an advantage on flights. At the moment you'll only have your eldest to watch, whereas in a couple of months you'll have two of them on the move.

If your older child is still sleeping in the afternoon, you can start to synchronize nap times from around 3 months as it's fairly easy to get your baby to have a long after-lunch nap from around now. Once you've settled your toddler, encourage your baby to sleep – rocking and singing if necessary – because if she falls asleep at the same time each day she'll start to become naturally tired at this time within about 4 days.

Likewise, you can synchronize bedtimes now that your baby is old enough to start having early nights. From 3 months she will start to become tired in the evenings, and this will increase over the next few weeks, making early nights increasingly easier to achieve.

TODDLER Ⓐ Ⓑ Ⓒ

Your toddler will be able to have much more fun with his baby sibling now that she's laughing and fascinated by the world. He can shake her baby gym, pass her toys, take them away (she's too young to object), tickle her, drum on her tummy and so on. She's becoming more robust by the day, so don't rush in to her rescue too quickly – you may assume she's terrified, but you're more likely to find that she's delighted by her older sibling's attention. Babies seem to adore the small faces and high-pitched voices of young children.

As well as having fun making his baby sibling laugh, your toddler can also become jealous around now as his baby sibling learns to flirt and charm with increasing skill. So when you find yourself giggling away with your baby, do include your toddler wherever possible. And also have similar giggling sessions with him.

When your baby charms strangers, friends and family, it can be particularly tough for your toddler as they will often completely ignore him while giving the baby masses of attention. As we've mentioned, you can try whispering conspiratorially, 'Everyone loves your sister/brother, don't they?' as this can sometimes take the sting out of jealous feelings because it gives your toddler a sense of ownership and therefore reflected glory. But you'll probably encounter a renewed bout of envy from your toddler, complete with extra demands for attention. Do give him plenty of one-to-one time, because at the end of the day he's the 'less cute' child, which can be very tough.

It's also important to be responsive to your baby. This is not only essential for her development but it's important for your toddler, too. He may be jealous but he would find it confusing if you ignored the baby in an attempt to keep his jealousy at bay. He needs to see you being loving to his sibling, and with luck he'll mimic your behaviour and be loving towards her, too. More importantly, lots of smiling and gurgling with your baby will help her to become more sociable and friendly, and this will make her more appealing to your eldest than if she were a cranky crier.

It's fair to say that babies are relatively easy to look after between the ages of 3 and 6 months because they're in a routine but they aren't yet mobile. So we suggest that you take advantage of this by embarking on a 3-month toddler training session, tackling any problems with eating, sleeping and so on before your baby becomes mobile. This is also a good window in which to potty-train – if your toddler is ready, of course. We're definitely advocates of child-led potty-training, so nothing too competitive such as trying to potty-train earlier or more quickly than friends. It's essential to take a relaxed approach. Then, with lots of encouragement and perhaps some stickers and rewards, your child will learn to use the potty quite easily once he's ready.

CHILD 😎

Because your baby has lost her infant floppiness, it will be much easier for your older child to hold her – supervised of course. And children aged about

6 years and upwards have the coordination and balance to be able to carry a baby – on carpeted floors and with supervision.

Encouraging your child to make the baby laugh will also help to develop their bond, just as with toddlers. But, just like toddlers, older children can become jealous now that their baby sibling is able to command increasing amounts of attention.

You may find that your child starts to really compete for your attention and that it's no longer enough to have your undivided attention when the baby is asleep. Instead, your child may start to demand your attention when the baby is awake, and you are then 'choosing' to spend time with him rather than the baby.

Your child may even start to resent you going off to put your baby down for a nap – perhaps he can hear you laughing together. You can avoid this by keeping communication low-key between you and your baby in preparation for her nap. If you try taking your child upstairs with you at the time of your baby's nap, he'll almost certainly make a nuisance of himself and, depending on his age and temperament, may climb into the baby's cot and generally be disruptive.

If this happens, your child is giving you a strong message that he wants you to choose and prioritize him over the baby. The more often you are able to do this, the calmer he will feel and the better he will behave. The obvious time is when Dad is around – then Dad can look after the baby, freeing you up to 'choose' to play with your eldest.

Some children are particularly easy-going and if they happen to have a demanding baby sibling they can get a little neglected. If this sounds like your child, he won't necessarily demand extra attention by misbehaving, or at least not just yet. Being aware of such a situation is a major step in resolving it – the solution is, of course, to spend one-to-one time with your eldest.

We've said already that your baby will be relatively easy to look after at the moment, so make the most of this and have fun with your eldest. If you go on outings and day trips you can take your baby along in her buggy, and because she's not yet mobile she'll have no desire to get out.

HOUSEKEEPING

Once your baby starts going to bed early you'll have your evenings back with your partner, and adult evening meals can once again be something to look forward to. You'll obviously be cooking for your eldest child at about 5 p.m., but there's no need to cook twice – once you've settled your children the last thing you'll feel like is cooking a meal from scratch. Here's how to get organized so that you can come down to a meal that you've 'prepared earlier'.

As a general rule, meals that you bake in the oven will still taste delicious a few hours later, so things like shepherd's pie, fish pie, macaroni cheese and pasta bakes work well – just heat them up in the oven for 20 minutes. Casseroles can be kept at a very low heat in the oven after you've served your toddler – the meat will get softer and softer and you can top the casserole up with liquid to stop it drying out. Pancakes are another option – you can add fillings and bake them later.

With some meals you'll need to cook one or two things separately later. Pasta, for example, always tastes better freshly cooked (unless it is baked), so if you're having spaghetti bolognaise you can heat up the sauce, prepared earlier, and cook the pasta from scratch. Likewise, some vegetables aren't very nice warmed up later, whereas others are fine. Here's a list to help with meal-planning:

- **Foods that taste OK re-heated:** frozen peas, spinach, cabbage, carrots, mashed potato or any other vegetable that is mashed, such as squash, celeriac and so on; couscous, rice (re-heat rice very thoroughly with a little water, and don't keep it for longer than a day to avoid food poisoning), lentils, butter beans and any other pulses. Curries and chilli con carne are all fine heated later, and you can convert them from children's food into adult food by adding soy sauce and chilli sauce. Likewise, you may need to use a salt cellar if you're keeping your toddler's salt intake to a minimum, as this can be a little bland for adult food.

- **Foods that don't:** broccoli, cauliflower, mangetout, green beans, sprouts, oven chips, baked potatoes and roast potatoes. Pan-fried meat and fish dry out if re-heated. And stir-fries go soggy – although you can get everything ready-chopped to be fried later.

   Rather than boiling vegetables and having to keep an eye on the stove, you can use a microwave steamer, which means you can leave the vegetables to cook while you do something else. It's also healthier to steam vegetables! The vegetables will take around 3 minutes to steam in the microwave, then stay hot for another 15 minutes. You can get everything ready in the steamer, then start the microwave just before story time. Your vegetables will be ready just as your children settle (at least in theory!).

SUNDAY ROAST

One oven dish that doesn't keep until later is a roast which, of course, relies on everything being timed carefully so that the meat, potatoes and vegetables are all ready to serve at the same time. So this is best kept to the traditional Sunday lunchtime slot, which is when most families choose to eat their roast.

There will be occasions when you won't want to cook just one meal, for example on the nights when you want to eat something a bit special – a good steak, for example – that your toddler wouldn't appreciate. Or perhaps your partner enjoys cooking, in which case he'll probably cook from time to time while you put the children to bed. Or you may be having people over for dinner. In this instance you can cook something quick for your toddler before cooking 'adult' food later.

Another way of organizing your cooking schedule is to prepare the main meal once the children are asleep, then give them a portion of it warmed up the next day. For example, roast chicken with mashed potatoes and peas is delicious served up the next day.

It's a matter of choosing what works for you, and this will probably vary from day to day depending on what's going on, such as what time your partner gets home, or what sort of mood your children are in.

TROUBLESHOOTING

I'm fed up with shopping online, but how do I get both children around the supermarket?

Some trolleys have a baby-and-toddler seat – take a blanket to line the baby seat and make it more comfortable. Alternatively you can put your baby in the baby carrier and your toddler in the trolley. Or you can push a double buggy and balance a small shopping basket on the handle, or a large laundry bag over the handle if you've got a lot of shopping to do. You won't get stopped for shoplifting – unless of course you walk out without paying!

As for keeping your baby and toddler happy, ensure your baby is well fed before you set off so there's a good chance she'll sleep. And allow your toddler (or older child) to choose one treat – you'll have to supervise his choice, of course. If he's under 2½ you'll probably have to give him his treat before you get to the checkout, because he's too young to understand waiting, but you can check the wrapper through the till and no one will mind. Another option is to give your toddler a 'picnic lunch' when you shop, so prepare some finger food such as sandwiches. Even adults find it hard to walk past aisles of food, so if your toddler is eating this may help. And avoid the confectionery aisles.

For an older child you can make supermarket shopping into a game by getting him to find items on the shelves and letting him throw any non-breakables into the trolley.

I feel exhausted and am usually too tired to play with my eldest

Try some child-led play where you simply watch your child play and make comments about what he's doing – such as, 'Ooh, you're finding all the red Lego bricks and adding them to your spaceship.' If your child asks you to do something, like find the blue bricks, co-operate. The idea is that he's in charge and also that you are concentrating solely on him and not trying to do anything else, like winding the baby. This has an extremely calming effect on children and you'll see results within just 15 minutes. Child-led play is a technique often used by therapists, and the theory is that doing something with a child has far more impact than talking. You may feel that you're helping your child by talking about his problems and frustrations, but often you can be just as helpful by playing with him.

After such a play session with your child you may find that you can sit feeding the baby while you watch him play, just giving the odd comment about what he is doing to show that you are interested.

My toddler is very affectionate with his baby sibling, but sometimes cuddles her so hard that she cries

Toddlers (and older children) generally feel mixed emotions towards their baby sibling, including affection and love as well as resentment and anger. They feel these positive and negative emotions all at the same time, and they don't know how to deal with them. A common response to these confused feelings is to hurt the baby subtly. So do watch out for hugs that start gently then suddenly become very rough, or rocking the baby chair so hard she gets upset, or tickling that starts to hurt. Try not to get cross; it's normal for children to hate their baby siblings.

As always, give lots of reassurance and one-to-one attention, but do state clearly that we have to be gentle with the baby. And watch carefully when your child is being affectionate towards the baby, as his feeling may suddenly change. Try not to jump in too soon – your baby will let you know as soon as she's unhappy – in the meantime it is safe to assume your toddler is being gentle, so do praise his kind behaviour.

CHAPTER 9
Months 6–12

Your baby will pass more big milestones during this 6-month period than at any other time in her life, as she learns to sit up, crawl, stand and perhaps walk a few steps and say a couple of words. She will also start on solid food and will soon be sitting in a high chair holding her own spoon.

This is certainly an exciting time but, when you've got another child, it does bring a whole new set of challenges. Thankfully there are plenty of steps you can take to make life a little easier. So in this chapter we'll be talking about how to deal with the inevitable jealousy as your eldest watches his baby sibling pass milestone after milestone, the challenge of your baby becoming mobile and needing constant watching, and coping when your baby starts to grab your older child's toys.

Although your days will become busier as your baby grows, your nights will hopefully become more settled – around 80 per cent of all 9-month-olds can sleep for at least 5 hours at night, and babies weighing 7.3 kg (16 lb) or more are capable of sleeping for 8 hours without a feed. So keep working on dropping night-feeds and encouraging your baby to settle herself to sleep with minimal help from you. The day when both children sleep through the night is getting closer.

Another factor that will make your days easier is that your baby will need fewer breastfeeds (or bottles), dropping from 5 to 2 a day by the time she is a year old. Yes, you'll have to endure slow and sometimes torturous meals as you wean your baby while trying to stop your eldest messing about with his food. But being able to feed your children together and not being tied to milk-feeds, especially if you are breastfeeding, will ultimately make life much simpler.

MUM

We tentatively mentioned exercise in Chapter 7, knowing the reality is that you probably won't even have thought about this.

But as a general rule the more you get out and about (assuming you walk and don't drive, of course), the more calories you'll burn. If you weigh 67 kg (10½ stone), you'll burn around 70 calories an hour watching TV, 190 calories walking slowly, and 350 calories walking briskly. You can add around 50 calories an hour for carrying a small baby, and also around 50 an hour if you're pushing a buggy on rough ground.

You'll burn plenty of calories walking for a long time at a comfortable pace. But if you want to increase fitness, you'll need to get out of breath – so walk briskly, ideally uphill pushing a double buggy laden with shopping. Going from unfit to fit is an unpleasant process because it requires hours of feeling puffed out and tired, and this is made particularly difficult if you're sleep-deprived. Also if your toddler insists on walking it won't be possible for you to exert yourself when you're out with your children. So it's hardly surprising that it takes so many mothers several years to regain their pre-baby fitness and figure. But if you're determined, you'll get there in the end, even if it seems pretty much impossible at the moment. For now, don't waste energy worrying or feeling guilty. Get out as much as you can because it will make you feel better, and if you walk slowly for long enough you'll still burn plenty of calories.

You could also look into crèche services at your local leisure centre – most take babies over 4 months. This can be a good motivational tool because once you have booked a place for your children you'll feel obliged to turn up and not make last-minute excuses about feeling tired, having a cold and so on.

As we've mentioned previously, Pilates is a particularly good class to sign up for because it will encourage you to do your pelvic floor exercises – essential after you've had your second baby (even if you've had two Caesareans, the weight of carrying two babies will still have taken its toll on your pelvic floor). Do note that cycling and swimming both put less strain on your pelvic floor than running or jumping.

A leaky bladder affects 1 in 4 women – becoming more likely with each baby you have, and also getting worse with age as your muscles lose tone. If you're leaking when you sneeze, jump or run, it's worth seeing your GP, who may suggest physiotherapy or even surgery. But for less serious cases, doing your pelvic floor exercises 3 times a day for 3 months will make a difference – pull your muscles inwards and upwards as though stopping yourself weeing and passing wind. This may sound like a long, tedious process but as well as stopping a leaky bladder these exercises will also improve your sex life resulting in longer, stronger orgasms as your muscles become more toned. The exercises will also improve vaginal tone, which increases sensation during sex.

Breastfeeding

As you wean your baby onto solids, you'll drop milk feeds – aim for 3 breastfeeds a day by 8 months, and of course none during the night. Giving your baby more milk than this will affect her appetite for solids. By 9 months your baby can have just 2 long feeds a day. If you return to work before this time, your baby can drink either expressed milk or formula at lunchtime.

If you are bottle-feeding you should continue with formula until your baby is a year old.

MARRIAGE PROBLEMS

Most couples find it a terrific strain going from one to two children, and will run into relationship problems from time to time. This is especially likely if your children are closely spaced, which is a growing trend as women are having children later in life and so having to race against their biological clock.

It's hard enough getting time alone with your partner when you have just one child, but with two this becomes more difficult. So book babysitters and persuade family members to help out whenever possible – even an hour on your own together can be invaluable. As a general rule, the more often you can find time to be on your own together, the less your relationship will be affected by having two young children.

Another thing that can help you through these tough times is to both have a wish list – identify the single thing you need each week that will help keep you sane during this tough period. This may include things like going for a drink with friends, having a lie-in or not having to cook for a day.

Once you've worked out your needs, tell your partner and negotiate – one of you may be desperate to have a lie-in, the other may crave a night out with friends. The key is to agree to a swap so that you both feel that some of your needs are being met and that your partner is looking after you.

Life will get easier as broken nights become rarer and you and your partner start to feel less exhausted and irritable.

BABY

Most babies start crawling between the ages of 7 and 10 months and, as you'll no doubt remember, you will need to watch your baby constantly to ensure she doesn't hurt herself or put small objects in her mouth.

From now your time will be more squeezed than ever. But there's lots you can do that will help.

First, the more you can adapt your home, the easier life will be. We talked about baby-proofing your house in Chapter 2, but if you didn't quite get around to doing this for your first child, make sure you do so now for your second. Not only will you have two children to watch, you may well get caught out by your baby's milestones. For example, she'll climb on a chair and reach things on the kitchen surface when you're least expecting it because you'll still think of her as your baby and forget that she's growing up all the time.

Be particularly careful with your older child's small toys and think about packing some away for a few months – for example Lego and Playmobil can be difficult because of the small parts, whereas Duplo and wooden train sets are fine as they are too big to fit in your baby's mouth (or at least to get down her throat!).

Consider a playpen. This not only keeps your baby safe from herself, but also safe from her elder sibling. If you keep it filled with interesting toys or objects that your baby hasn't played with for several days, she may be happy for up to 15 minutes at a time – long enough for you to go to the toilet, answer the door or even prepare a simple meal.

You can also present your baby with boxes of toys or objects that she hasn't seen before, or at least not for a few weeks – while she's busy exploring these she won't be on the move.

If your baby is having a particularly grizzly day, pop her in the sling, facing outwards. She may be happy for a while, cuddled up to you and watching the world from a different height.

PLACID BABIES

Do note that if your baby is particularly placid, she may accept being left in her bouncy chair. It's important that you give her plenty of 'floor time' out of the chair, though, as this is essential for muscle development – even though it's extra work for you having to watch her constantly. If you have another child it's particularly tempting to leave her for too long in her bouncy chair. With lively babies, this is no longer an option.

Going out can be a big relief during the baby-watching stage. At playgroup or any other activities you do, you'll now have to watch two children as your baby will no doubt want to crawl around and explore. Even if your baby crawls fast, usually from around 10 months, playgroup is a relatively easy environment in which to manage two young children because it is safe and there will be other adults on hand.

When you go to the playground, our advice is to leave your baby in her buggy for as long as possible, perhaps until she is a year old if you can get away with it. Once you get her out she'll want to do the same each time, which can be difficult, particularly if there's a close age gap between your children. So although your baby may be physically capable of going on a swing from 8 months, we suggest you leave her in the buggy for now but position her buggy where she can watch her sibling or other children playing – most babies will find this entertaining.

If your baby is very insistent that she wants to get out of her buggy and you really don't think you can manage, try going to the park when she is due for a nap – she's less likely to want to get out if she's tired, and may well fall asleep.

If your eldest child is aged 3 or older he will be reasonably independent and, depending on your particular playground, safe. If this is the case then you can let your baby enjoy the swings from an earlier age. Or you may still choose to leave her in the buggy for a little longer so you can sit on a park bench for 20 minutes and rest.

When Dad comes to the park it will be easy to manage both children so your baby can of course 'play' on the swings and so on. On these occasions, leave the buggy at home and put your baby in her carrier, then she'll learn to associate the carrier with 'getting out' and the buggy with 'staying in'.

Playtime

From around 7 months your baby will learn to sit up, and by about 8 months she'll be crawling, enabling her to have fun playing with her older sibling. She'll become fascinated by whatever her older sibling is doing, and will be keen to join in. Encouraging your children to play together is one of the best ways of helping them bond. With time they will start to entertain each other and start to need you less.

Here are some ideas:

- **Brick tower** – show your toddler or older child how to build a tower of bricks for your baby to bash down.

- **Soft ball** – your eldest can roll a large soft ball to your baby, who may be able to bash it back again in your toddler's direction.

- **Crawling** – your eldest child can demonstrate how to crawl through cardboard boxes – your baby will delight in copying him.

- **Doctors** – your baby can be the patient.

- **Shops** – your baby can be the shopkeeper – your eldest can take things and give them back to the baby (avoid toy money as it is a choking hazard).

- **Kitchens** – your baby can be a chef – if she's got her own box of kitchen bits to play with, she won't annoy her older sibling.

- **Play dough** – your baby will be happy to play with just a couple of cutters, but from about 16 months she will demand some play dough, too, as she becomes more observant.

- **Baking (with Mum)** – your baby will be happy in her high chair with a bowl and spoon, and a few other kitchen utensils to bash while your older child gets more involved in the cooking.

- **Story time** – choose board books when reading to both children because your baby will try to turn the pages like your older child. Paper books will be destroyed.

Toy-grabbing

From about 10 months your baby will grab your eldest's toys from time to time. Although annoying for your toddler, babies at this age can be easily fobbed off with an alternative toy. So teach your eldest to present the baby with a decoy (a toy he's not playing with) as she approaches. This will distract the baby from whatever her sibling happens to be doing. Also, if the baby has something that your toddler wants, all he has to do is swap it with something else. Your baby will willingly accept a swap at this age. Once your eldest has mastered these techniques, he'll be able to manage the baby's potentially annoying behaviour.

Make it clear that you sympathize with your eldest. And try to laugh together at the baby randomly grabbing at toys that are too old for her. The funnier your toddler finds this, the less likely he is to lose his temper and thump the baby.

BOTH UNDER 2 – WHEN YOUR CHILDREN
ARE NEARLY TWINS

If you've got a very close age gap you'll still be watching your toddler all the time because children need constant monitoring until they are about 2, then it is usually safe for you to be upstairs while your child is downstairs, or vice versa.

With very young, closely spaced children you'll now have to watch the two of them, which is obviously very challenging – and some would say harder than having twins, who are at least interested in the same things. But once your eldest reaches 2 you'll find it a lot easier to look after your children. Even reaching 18 months can make life a little less hectic, because at this age children start to develop their sense of danger and become slightly less likely to hurt themselves.

In the meantime try to accept mess, muddle, overflowing laundry baskets and not getting much done. It's only for a few months, and this really is as chaotic as parenting is ever going to be (unless you have more children of course!). The best thing you can do at this stage is to get down on the floor and play – it's relatively easy to keep your children happy at this age, and much easier to achieve than a tidy, organized home.

One of the advantages of having both children under the age of 2 is that they will have their lunchtime nap at the same time, which gives you time to yourself. Another advantage is that you can load them into a double buggy and go for long sanity-saving walks.

And finally, they will be incredibly sweet together. You've basically got a little baby and a giant baby, and watching them interact can be utterly charming. When you're out and about you'll often find yourselves the centre of attention, and hopefully get lots of support, often from complete strangers.

Mealtimes

You will probably wean your baby at 6 months, or perhaps earlier depending on current guidelines. Assuming you opt for 6 months, we suggest a method of mixed weaning, giving your baby both purees and finger food. In our opinion baby-led weaning (finger food only) is too time-consuming when you've also got a toddler. And the puree-only method isn't generally suitable when weaning a baby at 6 months, because you need to progress so quickly onto lumpy foods and iron-rich foods.

You may need to buy a second high chair for your baby, depending on the age of your eldest. As a general guide, children need a high chair until they are about 2½, then a toddler booster chair until they are about 4 to ensure that they are comfortable when they eat and not kneeling up on adult dining chairs.

Weaning will be slow initially because your baby will be spitting out lots of purees and baby rice. But by the time she is 9 months she will hopefully have moved on to eating 3 solid meals a day including mashes, purees and finger food. Avoid giving her soft-boiled, fried and poached eggs because of the risk of food poisoning. Other than that she can eat pretty much what your toddler eats – you can adapt her food to make it easier to eat so that you don't have to cook two separate meals for your children (see the 'Housekeeping' section for meal ideas on pages 128–29).

By the time your baby is a year old she should be eating the same food as the rest of the family, but avoiding potential choking hazards (for example grapes, nuts and cherries). And she'll need full-fat milk until she's 2.

You'll almost certainly find it easier to wean your baby this time than first time around. You'll know what you're doing and be much more relaxed whenever your baby decides not to eat – you'll simply try again at the next meal rather than waste time fretting. Now your challenge will be coping with your older child, who may well play up as he watches his baby sibling starting to eat solid food.

TODDLER 🄰🄱🄲

Your toddler is likely to become upset when he sees his baby sibling learning to crawl and starting to eat solids. He'll either misbehave or regress by insisting on crawling or being spoon-fed.

This happens because when your baby passes a new milestone she'll get lots of extra praise and attention, and your eldest child will have to endure listening to his baby sibling being called clever, good, and even big and grown-up. Added to this, he may start to perceive his younger sibling as a potential competitor – the milk-guzzling, immobile infant is becoming more like him by the day as she learns to eat with a spoon, crawl and perhaps even pull herself to standing. Thankfully there are steps you can take to avoid this becoming too much of an issue.

Regression

As we've said in previous chapters, regression is a classic response to a younger sibling's milestones, and the best thing you can do is play along. Your toddler will soon become bored, especially if you make a point of praising him for his advanced skills. So tell him that not only can he walk, he can also stand on one leg, jump and perhaps hop. Likewise, praise him for being able to use a knife and fork as well as a spoon. And point out that he's much better at getting his food into his mouth than his baby sibling is.

Misbehaviour

Positive praise and attention, and one-to-one play sessions are the most effective ways to rectify poor behaviour. But there will be occasions, usually at mealtimes, when your toddler doesn't want to be praised for being 'big' but instead smears his food over his face and drops his spoon and perhaps his entire meal on the floor – just like the baby. Resist the temptation to get cross as this would seem very unfair to him – after all, when the baby does such things you cheerfully mop up the mess.

So if you can grit your teeth and say, 'Oh dear, two messy babies today,' then change the subject quickly, it will de-power your toddler's behaviour and he'll be less likely to do it again.

It's really worth staying in control when this phase occurs, because if you lose it, your toddler will not only be pleased with the attention, he'll get lots of satisfaction from your anger. Before you know it you'll have created a mealtime battleground that can become increasingly out of control.

AVOID CHOKING

Ensure that your eldest doesn't put finger foods into your baby's mouth as this could lead to choking, or at the very least will annoy her. Unless your baby can pick up food and eat it by herself, she probably won't be able to chew and swallow it. A baby's manual dexterity keeps pace with her ability to manage food in her mouth.

TV Temptation

If your eldest no longer has an afternoon nap you may well be tempted to pop him in front of the television while your baby sleeps. Thirty minutes of television while you settle the baby for her nap and get a few things done won't do your toddler any harm as long as he's over 2. Just be aware that once you introduce the TV at a certain time of day, your toddler will come to expect it. And then there's the temptation to let your toddler watch TV for the full duration of your baby's nap – 2 hours or more. This is easily done – you'll suddenly hear your baby crying and realize the time has flown and your eldest is still watching television. Try not to let this happen, because lots of mums find that their children don't behave as well when they've watched a lot of television. Likewise with Game Boys and iPads – while these may be useful 'babysitters', they won't benefit your child in the slightest and plenty of mums have found they make their children more aggressive. In an ideal world children wouldn't play on these until they are much older.

We advise that you have at least 15 minutes one-to-one time with your toddler while your baby is sleeping. The more time you can give him, the happier and calmer he will be. After some one-to-one time, children are often happy to play by themselves for a while.

As well as playing with your toddler, you can involve him in your chores – cooking is a particularly popular activity for young children, but you could also experiment with washing the floor, helping with the laundry and so on. It may take more time and energy to make mundane tasks fun, but it will save you time and energy later if your toddler doesn't misbehave through lack of attention.

STARTING NURSERY

If your eldest is about to start nursery you may be given a choice of mornings or afternoons. Consider the following to help you make your choice:

- Afternoons usually coincide with your baby's long nap, so this will give you time at home on your own.

- Mornings will tire out your toddler, meaning that he'll be happy to play calmly at home in the afternoons.

- And think about what your friends with young children are doing, and whether you want to continue your morning activities with your toddler or perhaps prefer to do them just with your baby.

CHILD 😁✓

Just like toddlers, older children can become jealous when their baby sibling passes a milestone. As always, lots of praise will help. You can also get your child involved – for example playing crawling games with the baby, and helping at mealtimes. From about the age of 4 your child will have the dexterity to spoon-feed your baby – he'll soon tire of this activity, but being involved may help him feel less jealous. Ensure he uses a soft spoon just in case he becomes over-zealous – his feelings are liable to flip within seconds from being very caring to being angry with the baby, and for no apparent reason.

If helping out isn't enough to ease his jealousy and he messes about at the table, you'll need to follow a slightly stricter, age-appropriate strategy than the one we give for toddler mealtime messing about.

As with a toddler, you can indulge any mealtime regression initially by mopping up spills cheerfully. But follow this with a gentle warning: 'Big children don't spill food unless it's an accident.' He's given you a test to see if you love him as much as the baby, and your kind, patient response will hopefully reassure him.

However, if your child continues to mess about, don't indulge him anymore but calmly warn him that you'll take his food away, and then take it as soon as he misbehaves again. This may lead to angry tears and perhaps a tantrum, but be strong and also resist giving him extra snacks to fill up on before his next meal. And always ensure that your child is hungry before a meal, so resist pleas for snacks at least an hour before mealtimes. Within about 3 days he'll have learned not to mess about at the table.

This sounds simple on paper, but we know the reality is very hard. We urge you to stay calm and not give in, however furious or upset your child becomes. You may prefer a softer style of parenting using gentle negotiation – this can work well for some families, but the downside is that it is more time-consuming and it's easy to lose patience and end up yelling. If this happens then it's definitely worth considering the stricter approach.

Even if your child's table manners improve, you can expect clowning about at the table to recur time and time again over the years now that you have more than one child. This is obviously tedious and can spoil a family meal. But follow our strategy of giving a warning before taking away food, and then occasionally you will be rewarded with fun family conversation and beautifully behaved children. In the meantime, try to resist the very tempting alternative of ready meals. And remind yourself you're not alone – the family table plan in households with more than one child invariably seats children separately, quite often one each end of the table.

Bathtime

As we said in Chapter 7, it can be fun for your children to bath together once your baby reaches about 10 months and can sit up and play. But don't force this if your older child isn't keen, because from as young as 4 children can start to feel modest from time to time. You may find that sometimes your eldest wants to bath with his sibling, and on other nights he wants privacy and to bath alone. Allow him to choose.

HOUSEKEEPING

Room-sharing

At 6 months your baby no longer needs to sleep in your bedroom, so your children may start sharing a room from around now. Give your eldest plenty of warning and try to sell the idea by talking about what fun it will be. You could also buy him new bedding or pyjamas to mark the moving-in occasion, and put up a shelf for his special toys to keep them out of reach of the baby.

Allow about a week for your children to become used to sharing a room – at first it is almost bound to take longer for them settle and go to sleep, but this will speed up as they become used to each other. There are various ways you can settle them to sleep.

The ideal way is to kiss them both goodnight at the same time, then leave the room to let them drift off to sleep. In reality you may find that they distract and disturb each other, especially as they get older. If this is the case you can stay in the room, perhaps tidying or even telling a story until one of them drifts off to sleep. Or you can keep your eldest up a little later – 15 minutes is usually enough time for your youngest to either fall asleep or at least become too sleepy to be distracted by your eldest when he comes to bed. If you do this, you'll have to teach your eldest that stories and other settling rituals don't take place in the bedroom. But it should be easy enough to persuade him to accept the new routine if you emphasize that he's staying up later because he's so 'big and grown-up'.

Meals Suitable for a Baby and a Toddler

There's no need to slavishly cook two meals – here are some foods that both babies and older children can eat, and tips on how to make a few simple adaptations to make some of the foods baby-friendly:

- Pancakes
- Omelettes – cut into strips for your baby to eat with her fingers
- Eggy bread (bread dipped in egg and fried) – again cut it into strips
- Scrambled egg – don't overdo the milk and it will be easier to pick up
- Baked potatoes – scoop out the middle and mash with milk for your baby
- Chicken drumsticks – remove skin for your baby, or, to make it even easier, remove the meat for her
- Fish cakes and fish fingers – these can be mashed with a little milk
- Shepherd's pie – your baby's portion will need a bit of mashing, and don't give her any crispy topping
- Spaghetti bolognese – cut up the spaghetti into small pieces with scissors, and you may need to liquidize the minced beef as it can sometimes be quite hard and chewy

- Lasagne – chop it up with scissors and avoid giving your baby any crispy topping

- Oven chips – you can microwave these instead of baking them to make them super-soft (and a little soggy…)

- Meat – chop into tiny pieces. Liver and kidneys are particularly soft if you don't overcook them.

- Fish – shallow fry fillets of fish dipped in egg and flour and cut into batons. And you can dip tuna steaks into ground cumin before shallow frying to disguise strong fishy tastes (supermarkets sometimes sell fresh tuna pieces for half the price of tuna steaks).

- Satsumas and oranges – the segments need to be peeled until your baby is about a year old. It's a good idea to peel all fruit initially, as it can be difficult for babies to cope with peel.

Reducing the mealtime blitz

Another way to save time is to serve food that is easier to clean up:

Messy	Quicker to clear up
grated parmesan	parmesan flakes
grated cheese	sliced cheese
rice	pasta
kedgeree	pasta bake
mash	oven chips
mince	meatballs
runny yoghurt	set yoghurt (less likely to spill)
full cup of milk* or juice	3 centimetres of water

* Children need milk, of course, but you can give it to them in a cup with a lid.

TROUBLESHOOTING

Who do I go to first when both my children are crying?

We talked about this in Chapter 6 and suggested prioritizing your toddler. This was partly because your baby would probably be crying for a feed or because of wind – both of these take a while to resolve. Now that she's older she may cry because of something that you can sort out in seconds, such as not being able to reach a toy, or wanting a drink. Pre-verbal frustrated crying is often instantly resolved (assuming, of course, you can guess what your baby is 'saying'), so deal with this before tending to your toddler, who you can then spend longer with.

My toddler keeps trying to pull his baby brother's willy in the bath

This is fairly standard and certainly nothing to worry about. Siblings become increasingly repelled by each other with age, and from about 4 onwards the tiniest touch can lead to protests of 'germs'. So the problem of bathtime willy-pulling and trying to touch wee holes or bottom holes will naturally resolve itself. In the meantime you can gently discourage such activities by explaining that willies and wee holes are sensitive and we don't want to hurt each other – we can touch our own willy/wee hole but not other people's. Don't overreact by being shocked, and don't laugh, as this is guaranteed to result in a repeat performance. Try to react in the same way you would if your children had sloshed lots of water over the bathroom floor – a mildly-annoyed, don't-be-silly-it's-time-to-calm-down sort of reaction.

I've got a big age gap between my children as my eldest is now 6 and has plenty of attitude. I find that mums of younger children can be very disapproving

This is a classic scenario. Mothers of younger children haven't yet experienced how defiant children can be as they get older. Some mothers of younger children will no doubt judge you and what they consider to be your lack of parenting skills, which can be very frustrating and upsetting. There's not a solution for this situation, but there are two things we can say that will make you feel better. First, they'll learn. And secondly, the more judgemental a mother is, the more insecure about her own ability as a mother she is likely to be.

On a more practical note, when you visit people who aren't especially tolerant, ensure that your child has had some exercise and isn't ravenous. This will probably improve his behaviour, but there are, of course, no guarantees as children are notoriously unpredictable and oblivious to etiquette. Having said that, basic manners go a long way in counteracting less favourable behaviour. So we suggest that you work hard in teaching your child to always say 'please' and 'thank you', without being prompted.

CHAPTER 10
The Second Year and Beyond...

Congratulations, you've got through your first year with two children! Although in the second year the challenges continue, it won't be nearly as tiring because your baby will be sleeping much better at night, and also you'll be far more adept at managing two children.

The second year will certainly be busy as your baby learns to walk and talk, and your older child will no doubt find these milestones unsettling. But your children will start to have fun together this year. And by the time your baby reaches 18 months they'll actually start to squabble as your baby will be old enough to compete for both toys and your attention. The issue of sibling rivalry is vast and complex, which is why we've devoted an entire chapter to it (Chapter 11).

As the years pass and your children grow, you will no doubt have days, or at least a few hours, when things go rather well – there's no crying, you don't feel exhausted and your home is calm, happy and harmonious. But it's unrealistic to expect family life to run like a Disney film all the time.

There isn't a magic answer when it comes to parenting, and if you try and find one you'll end up feeling frustrated and thinking that you're doing something wrong. The reality is that you'll be constantly striving to be calmer and more organized, and that you'll be forever adapting your parenting style and techniques to meet your children's ever-changing needs.

Although parents of older children will no doubt tell you that this is the 'easy stage' as they watch you struggling with a tantrumming toddler and a teething baby, then helpfully add, 'just wait until they're teenagers,' we truly believe that your children will never be as physically exhausting and all-consuming as when they are very little.

Already life will be easier than a year ago, and this will continue. Of course there are still plenty of challenges ahead – arguing, sibling punch-ups, your children concealing the truth and starting school, to name but a few. But none of these requires anything like the amount of physical energy and time you need to manage two tiny children.

✚ IMMUNIZATIONS ✚

Your youngest will be due to have her booster immunizations at 12 months, and her MMR vaccine at 13 months. Tell her what's going to happen – she's old enough to understand some of what you say. And also explain to your eldest about his sibling's upcoming vaccination if you're bringing him along to her appointment. Otherwise he may find it distressing when his baby sibling cries.

SIGNS THAT YOUR CHILDREN ARE FINALLY GROWING UP

The more closely spaced your children are, the more of a feeling of freedom and lightness you will experience:

- the last nappy, milk feed and lunchtime nap
- you no longer have to pack spare clothes, wipes and snacks every time you go out

- you can feed your children half an hour later than their mealtime without their world coming to an end

- they no longer freak out whenever you get a babysitter

- when you put your children to bed late, you won't pay for your decision every minute and second of the following day

- when you go out, you can rely on your children to wait for you at roads, so you no longer have to bellow at them to stop as they're running ahead of you

- public tantrums become very rare, because between the ages of 4 and 6 children develop social awareness, so would usually be too embarrassed to start shouting furiously in public.

MUM

We've not covered going back to work until now, because it's quite common to take an entire year off when you have a second child as this gives you extra time with your firstborn. And plenty of mums decide not to return to work at all after their second child. Sometimes it's not financially viable to go back to work, given the cost of childcare for two children.

When doing your sums on whether it is worth returning to work, do bear in mind that childcare costs will lessen once your children start nursery, because nurseries are government-subsidized for children from 3 years old. And school will mean free childcare from 9 a.m. until 3.30 p.m. – assuming you use the state system, of course. But even when your children are at school, you may need to make childcare arrangements for them to be dropped off and picked up, as school days are shorter than the working day. You'll also need cover for the school holidays. When applying for schools, do plan long-term, as some schools are more geared towards working parents than others with breakfast and after-school clubs each day.

Getting ready for work can be tricky when you have small children, and will take longer than when you just had one child. Plenty of mothers use the television in the morning, as it allows them to get ready in peace. One option is to reward your children with watching a TV programme once they have had breakfast and are dressed and ready to leave. This will give you about half an hour to yourself. Or you could get yourself ready before your children are up – though this isn't realistic if your children are very early risers.

When you get home from work, try to acknowledge your children simultaneously so that no one feels left out (and don't forget your partner!). Always treat both of your children with affection even if one ignores you while the other rushes over to hug you. On paper this is obvious, but when you're coming through the front door tired after work, it's easy to get it wrong.

Breastfeeding

Your baby should be having 2 feeds a day plus a cup of cow's milk to get her used to the taste. There's no need to stop breastfeeding yet, as your baby will continue to benefit. But some mums decide to stop breastfeeding after about a year. If you do, ensure your baby has 400ml (just under a pint) of cow's milk a day, including the milk on her cereal. She can drink the rest from a cup. This amount of milk will ensure that she is having enough calcium without spoiling her appetite for solids. If she's not keen on drinking cow's milk, your baby can have 3 or 4 small portions a day of calcium-rich food including cheese, yoghurt, pulses and cow's milk on her cereal. You can also follow these guidelines if your baby is bottle-fed.

BABY

From the age of about 1, your baby will begin to hero-worship her elder sibling, wanting to play with the same toys, eat the same foods and do the same activities, including riding a bike or skateboard – she's far too young, of course, but she'll want to try. She'll have a wonderful time trying to join in with his games, which will become easier as she learns to walk and talk.

This 'copycat' phase will intensify as she approaches the age of 2, when she'll refuse to put her shoes on or sit down to eat until her older sibling does so. If you've been used to getting your youngest ready first because she puts up the least resistance, you'll have to switch strategies and get your oldest into the bath first, or to put his coat on first.

Do capitalize on the copycat phase. It can be extremely useful for encouraging your youngest to co-operate with teeth-cleaning, feeding herself with a spoon, drinking from a cup and, eventually, potty-training. For example, your youngest is very likely to sit on the potty, climb onto the toilet or announce 'wee-wee coming' when she's far too young to go without nappies. But she'll have an excellent understanding of the theory by the time she's physically ready.

Between 12 and 18 months, separation anxiety peaks, and this can make babies very clingy – not easy when you've got two children. You may notice that your baby becomes upset when you pick up your eldest child. Although she appears jealous, she's actually concerned that you're not available to look after her because you're with another child – separation anxiety is a primeval response to ensure babies don't get left behind by their mothers. So your baby isn't being manipulative; she's genuinely anxious and you'll need to reassure and cuddle her.

From around 18 months your baby will be capable of deliberately provoking her older sibling, and will no longer be fobbed off with any old toy. Instead, if she wants something she'll be determined to get it. Likewise, if she decides that it's fun to break up a railway track, she'll keep on trying. And she'll relish the reaction she gets, however negative.

Babies also develop aggression from around this age, and will be far more likely to hit, kick or even bite their own sibling rather than other children. Even a very placid baby is quite likely to bite an older sibling. She's not doing this because she hates him, or even wants to hurt him. She's enraged and is acting impulsively – quite possibly because he's teasing her by not letting her have a toy.

Biting is quite likely to continue from time to time until your baby is about 3, when most children stop. In the meantime you can manage the situation, but you probably won't 'solve' it.

Watch out for the signs – a clenched jaw and lots of winding up by your eldest. If your baby bites, or hurts your eldest in any way, give him lots of comfort, just as you would to your baby. Then explain to your baby that 'We don't bite because it hurts.' Don't let your baby have the toy that she bit for – she shouldn't be rewarded. But nor should she be punished. At this age it would be a waste of time and not appropriate (however, for the sake of your eldest, you should be seen to 'tell her off'). Stay calm and consistent, and thankful that you don't have to deal with other mothers – usually the worst thing about biting incidents.

Until your baby is 2½ she'll have no understanding of the concept of sharing. So you'll need to manage her playtimes when your eldest is around. The best way is to get down on the floor and play with both your children, ensuring that your baby doesn't annoy her older sibling. Here are some ideas:

- Building games – while your eldest is busy, perhaps building a train set, give your youngest a specific 'job' such as finding all the people who are going to ride on the train. To ensure that your eldest is able to play undisturbed, you'll end up giving your youngest more attention. But to ensure your eldest doesn't become jealous, comment on what he is doing from time to time, making him feel important.

- Hide and seek – you and your youngest hide together – the little one will inevitably be noisy, making it easier for your eldest to find you both. Then you swap and your eldest hides (usually in the same place every time).

- Chasing games – you and your youngest chase your eldest, perhaps pretending to be a lion (children learning to talk can usually make animal noises before learning to say words).

- Jigsaws – your youngest can do a four-piece puzzle while your eldest works on something more difficult. They will both feel proud of their efforts. And your youngest is unlikely to interfere with her older sibling's jigsaw because she's happy to be 'grown-up' and do her own.

- Pretending games (such as Mummies and daddies) – your eldest decides who plays which character, and your youngest will be happy to co-operate. The key is for you to join in, too – it is such fun for small children to have an adult playing imagination games that they are unlikely to feel cross or squabble with each other.

- Stories – we mentioned reading board books to your children in the last chapter. But as your baby approaches 2 years old, she'll start to enjoy stories more and more and be far less likely to grab the books and rip them. So you'll be able to read stories to both your children at the same time. They can each choose a book then all snuggle down together. This works even if your eldest is as old as 5. Older children are happy to enjoy babyish books, especially at bedtime when they are tired, or perhaps they like the comfort of hearing some of their baby stories again.

- Bath games – when your baby is able to sit up reliably in the bath, usually sometime after 10 months, by which time she'll have the core strength to be able to pull herself to standing, she can have a lovely time playing in the bath with her older sibling. Give them plenty of bath toys – there's no need to buy these as you can use plastic beakers and bottles. Then let your children have fun together. Never discourage a happy water fight, as this boosts water confidence.

- If you get your baby out of the bath first, you can get her dry and ready for bed in the bathroom while your eldest continues to play in the bath. Then your baby can have a play while you take your eldest out of the bath. But if your baby is particularly adventurous and you find it stressful leaving her unsupervised, you could get your eldest out of the bath first and ready for bed in the bathroom. Then he can play by himself while you sort out the baby. This way the only time she'll be on her own is safely in the bath, with you right next to her.

IDOLIZING AN OLDER SIBLING

This is very common, especially if your children are the same sex. In many ways it's rather charming, but it's important that your youngest child develops her own identity. So find things that she's especially good at, and praise her for them. And as she gets older, encourage her to develop her own interests. Avoid the temptation to compare her with her older sibling – so easy to do, but something to watch as it isn't good for a child's self-esteem.

Fussy Eating

Fussy eating is notorious at this age, particularly from about 18 months. But this time you'll have the added problem of your eldest declaring that certain foods are 'yuk'. Whenever your eldest refuses a type of food, so does your youngest – she'll probably refuse to even try it. So serve your baby 'yuk' foods first and place her high chair far enough away from your eldest to prevent him from making negative comments. Alternatively you can give her such foods when your eldest is out. It's important that your youngest doesn't miss out on certain foods, or she too will grow up not liking them.

There is an upside to this situation in that it can work in reverse. If your eldest is happy to munch away on raw red pepper, give it to him first. Let your youngest watch for a while, then give her some to try. She'll almost certainly put it in her mouth, but it may take several more offerings before she makes a final decision that this is a food she is happy to eat.

Going to the Playground

Your local park is a great place to take two small children, and from the age of about 1 there's little chance of your baby accepting being left in her buggy. The best thing you can do for her development, and enjoyment of course, is to let her explore. You'll need to stay with her, especially before 18 months when her curiosity will outweigh her judgement. While doing this you'll also have to watch your older child, to both check he is safe and also be his audience – he'll want your attention more than ever now that you're with his younger sibling.

Survival Tips

- Swings are a good vantage point – while you push your youngest in a toddler swing (one with a safety cradle the child sits in), position yourself to be able to watch your eldest. And if your eldest happens to fall, you can dash over and scoop him up, leaving your youngest in her swing for a minute.
- Enclosed sandpits are also useful, because again you can dash across to rescue your eldest while leaving your youngest safely contained for a moment.
- Roundabouts allow you to ride with both children – your baby on your knee and your toddler on his own from about 3, when he'll be able to climb on and off by himself.
- Take a toy buggy for your youngest to push – this will keep her away from the climbing frame for a few minutes, giving you a chance to be with your eldest.
- Get your baby into the habit of eating snacks while she's still strapped in her buggy – again, this will buy you a few minutes with your eldest.
- Dress your children appropriately. For example, if they are wearing waterproofs and wellington boots, you won't mind when they jump in puddles. This will save you the bother of dashing over, not to mention reduce your stress.

Delayed Language Development

Research has found that second-born children generally learn to talk later than first-borns. This is thought to be because they have less one-to-one time with Mum and Dad, meaning that first-borns tend to reach the 50-word milestone earlier than second or subsequent children. But second-born children have been found to be more advanced in their conversational skills initially. This is probably as a result of listening to conversations between their siblings and parents – easier to understand than adult conversation but more complicated than pointing out individual words such as 'dog', 'cat' or 'tree'.

What is clear is that these early differences soon disappear. So there's no need to worry or try to do anything to iron out the differences. You only need to be concerned if your baby doesn't seem to understand simple words from about a year old, and hasn't said a single word by 18 months old. If this happens, get her checked out. If she has delayed language, it's unlikely to be due to her position in the family.

TODDLER 🄰🄱🄲

Most toddlers love being hero-worshipped by their baby sibling, as it makes them feel grown-up and boosts their self-esteem. So do point out how much the baby loves and admires your toddler. And if you emphasize how big he is, perhaps by getting him to demonstrate to the baby how well he puts his shoes on, you'll encourage him to be a bit more co-operative, which will of course make life a little easier.

But having a baby sibling aged between 18 months and 2½ can be extremely tough for your eldest, because babies this age are still too young to share or to 'play nicely', but they are certainly old enough to be a nuisance.

It is almost inevitable that your toddler will lose his temper and thump his younger brother or sister from time to time. But it's important not to automatically take your baby's side when this happens. Of course she'll need comforting, and of course you'll need to explain to your toddler that even if the baby annoys him, he mustn't hurt her. But do take the time to listen to his side of the story. Your toddler will be far less likely to hurt the baby next time she breaks up his track than if you'd yelled at him and perhaps punished him by taking his toy away. This would have made him resent the baby even more.

You can manage this situation by setting your toddler up to play at a table, or perhaps in his room – out of the way of the baby. You can also encourage him to tell you when the baby is annoying him. This allows you to sort out the situation before it develops rather than letting him resolve it his way, which would probably be by hitting the baby.

You can show him how to make the baby's destructive tendencies into a game. For example, he has to build a brick tower as high as he can before the baby bashes it down.

When the baby is being particularly annoying or perhaps aggressive, and your toddler has managed not to retaliate, reward him with a promise of playing together once the baby is asleep. This is a good opportunity for him, and you, to play with something that isn't suitable for babies – small Lego or a simple board game, for example.

The developmental gap between your children will shrink as your baby gets older and is able to do more, which will make playing together increasingly more fun for them. By the time your youngest is about 2, your children will be conspiring together and will find it hilarious when they get told off. There will be chasing games, jumping on beds, yells of 'poo poo', climbing on sofas and rolling on the floor (especially if you have two boys).

Your toddler will be delighted when you tell your youngest off – something he's probably not used to as it's hard to tell off a child who's under the age of about 2. And your youngest may like being told off initially as it's a rite of passage, showing that she's growing up.

Noise

Your household will become very noisy because, from about 2½, children love to shout and scream as a way of releasing pent-up energy. Shouting is usually driven by excitement rather than anguish, and just about all little children love to make a noise, especially when they get excited together. Don't make too much of this or it will become an attention-seeking device.

Of course there are times when it's totally inappropriate to shout, for example during a wedding ceremony or in the doctor's waiting room. But if you've not made too much fuss about shouting at other times, your children are more likely to be quiet when you specifically ask them to.

If you find the shouting particularly hard to tolerate, you could introduce the idea of 'inside' and 'outside' voices. Or perhaps only allow children to be noisy in certain areas of your home.

But sometimes your children will abandon any house rules and rush around making so much noise that they seem almost 'high' with excitement. They won't hear you telling them to calm down, let alone obey you, and the closer they are in age, the more this is likely to happen.

When you can't stand another second, divide and rule. Take one of them by the hand and lead him away to do something else. Once your children are separated they will calm down within minutes. If over-excitement becomes an issue, you can develop strategies to separate your children during the stressful moments of your daily routine, for example bedtime and getting ready for school. By sending one of them away to do his teeth, you'll calm the situation down almost instantly in the morning.

Your household is unlikely to become more peaceful as your children get older, but it will start to sound much happier because children cry less, particularly after the age of about 4. And by the time they are 6, children rarely cry at all, and will only do so if they are hurt or upset about something specific.

CHILD 😊

Much of what we've said in the Toddler section of this chapter applies to an older child as well. But it's also worth mentioning that a slightly older child will be able to teach his baby sibling different skills, such as walking, painting and even football. Most children won't have the patience to give a lesson longer than about 5 minutes, but it is worth encouraging as it is very good for the older one's ego and a lovely bonding experience for both children.

ONE-TO-ONE TIME

We've emphasized the importance of spending time alone with your eldest throughout this book. The need for individual parental time never goes away. When your baby is young and having daytime naps, we've suggested using this time to play with your older child. But as your 'baby' grows up and finally drops all her naps (at about 3 years), one option is to stagger bedtimes by about 15 minutes. This way, your 'baby' also gets one-to-one time with you.

While you settle your youngest, older children are usually happy to play by themselves, because they know that they're about to get you all to themselves. This is just one option for planning one-to-one time into a family schedule, but there are plenty of other ways of doing it. For example, if you can arrange for your children to attend after-school clubs on different nights, then you'll have at least half an hour with the non-clubbing child before you have to pick up the 'clubber'. This only works if you don't work full-time and live near to the school. An alternative is to take children out for special one-to-one treats – this would have to be regular so that each child knows that his turn is definitely coming. Or if one of your children has a play date or a party, make a point of playing with his sibling while he is away.

HOUSEKEEPING

If your children share a bedroom, you'll need to think about how to give them their own space. From the age of about 4 or 5, children start to become territorial and want to keep their things separate. Here's how:

1. Bunk beds – your eldest can sleep in a top bunk from the age of about 4, when he'll be competent enough at climbing to be able to go to the toilet in the night if he needs to. Bunk beds give children their own private space to play (especially the top bunk, which can be kept out of bounds from younger siblings). And the bunks also give children their own wall space to decorate. You can also put up a shelf next to each bunk.

2. Shelves – children like to have their own private possessions from about the age of 4½, and will start to collect small, cheap toys. Give them their own shelf that is out of bounds to their siblings – initially because the shelf is too high. And once the youngest child is old enough to reach, she's also old enough to understand she's not allowed to touch. If you have bunk beds you can position these shelves next to each bunk to give your children extra 'territory'.

3. Lock-up boxes – a cash box with its own combination lock (from office supply shops) can be used by children from about the age of 5 to store favourite 'treasures'. They will love the sense of privacy because no one else can open their box. One tip here is to keep a copy of the combination lock number – otherwise you'll spend a long time trying different combinations to open the box when your child inevitably forgets the correct number.

4. Have communal space and toys. This is important or you will end up creating a battleground. Most toys should be shared unless there is a good reason not to – for example it's not fair to share a carefully constructed Lego model which would get broken, so this should

be kept on the 'shelf'. If you encourage a system of shared toys, explaining that sharing everything gives everyone twice as many toys to play with, your children will grow up accepting this. For this reason we don't recommend putting locks on cupboards – and there's always the risk that your children will lock each other inside.

5. If you've got a boy and girl sharing, keep the décor neutral – primary colours can work well, or stick to white with perhaps yellows or greens. Letting your children choose their own duvet covers gives them the opportunity to stamp their individuality and preference on their surroundings, but without dominating the room.

6. Divide the room by time: Let one child in to play by themselves, then let the other have a turn. This isn't for every day, but there will be occasions when your children need time and space on their own.

7. Clever lighting: As your children get older, one may like to read or draw in bed while the other sleeps. A small, focused reading light can usually be used without disturbing the other child, especially if they are used to sleeping with a night light rather than in pitch dark.

8. Play dates: If you have friends over to play you can avoid them fighting over the bedroom by having one child over at a time and distracting your other child with a baking or messy craft session with you.

Choosing to Share a Bedroom

Lots of parents who have enough space for separate bedrooms still choose to put their children in the same room when they are young. This not only gives you an extra room, but gives your children more time together. It can be a good option if both your children go to nursery, where they may be separated during the day due to their age difference. It will boost their bond to share bedtime stories, chatter after lights out and see each other as soon as they wake up.

The other advantage is that it can make the bedtime routine easier and more relaxing when your children are very young, as you can read stories to both of them at once and get them calm and settled together. This makes it easier to do bedtime on your own rather than relying on your partner.

TROUBLESHOOTING

Sometimes my children wind me up so much that I hate them, and then feel really guilty

This is quite normal. We all have days with our children that are so horrendously stressful that we end up shouting at them, hating them and perhaps even fantasizing about locking them in a padded cell or walking out of the front door. If this hasn't happened to you yet, be warned, it probably will. But don't worry, it's entirely normal, especially when you've got more than one child, and they get to 4 or 5 and start arguing and answering back, or deliberately pushing your buttons.

You may also be pushed beyond your limit if one of your children is sleeping badly and you're exhausted, or perhaps you're stressed about something that has nothing to do with your children, such as work or relationship problems.

Feelings like this towards your children are rarely discussed, so you can be left feeling guilty and isolated. But take comfort knowing that such feelings are fleeting and temporary, and are unlikely to mean you're a dangerous parent, or even a bad parent – you're just stressed. Humans are aggressive by nature, and *feeling* violent is very different to *being* violent. The fact that you've felt aggressive rage towards your children and have managed not to act on it shows considerable self-restraint.

When you have one of these hate-filled, angry days, spend a few minutes watching your children once they are asleep. They will look small, young and vulnerable, and your loving, protective feelings will be instantly restored.

You'll no doubt feel guilty, but use this guilt to increase your resolve to find ways of making your life less stressful. It may be something simple such as going for a run or having more early nights – tiredness makes us irritable.

You can also reflect on how you could better handle such a situation next time, or even avoid such a stressful situation occurring in the first place. For example, if hair-washing at bathtime causes out-of-control tantrums, don't wash your children's hair unless you have help. Or, if that's not possible, don't wash both children's hair on the same night.

Don't waste *too* much time feeling guilty. Parents, after all, are human and we have our limitations – it simply wouldn't be natural to feel gentle, calm love towards our children all the time.

When to Get Help

There will almost certainly be times when you don't manage to control your aggression and you lose control – either verbally or physically. Just about all parents do this occasionally. But if this starts to happen more often, you need to seek help. Go and see your GP – whereas friends and family are likely either to judge you or tell you everything is fine, your doctor will be keen to get to the root of the problem. You may be depressed or just need more support.

CHAPTER 11
Sibling Rivalry

Constantly refereeing your children can be truly nerve-jangling. But sibling jealousy is a normal part of family life, and it's important that we let go of any dreams we may have of our children always playing happily together.

Some parents believe that they must be permanently calm and serene in front of their children if they are to get along. In theory this may help a bit, but the reality is that you'll yell – and end up feeling guilty when you yell – and you'll blame yourself and feel like a failure whenever your children don't get on. This in itself can make us more uptight and stressed than if we weren't trying so hard in the first place.

It's important to embrace a less ideal, more realistic version of family life and to know that the feelings of jealousy and competitiveness that humans have towards their brothers and sisters are primal and instinctive, and something we may never grow out of. As a parent you can't 'solve' sibling rivalry; instead, you learn to manage it. Once we can accept that sibling rivalry is a part of being human, we will feel less wound up by it. So when our children fight we're less likely to lose the plot, and hopefully we won't come down quite as hard on them – this instantly makes our homes more relaxed, and perhaps even a little more harmonious.

In fact, if managed cleverly, you can certainly reduce the level of fighting among your children. In this chapter we look at how to stop your children fighting quite so much in the first place – and how to help them when they do.

OUR RELATIONSHIP WITH OUR CHILDREN

This has a big impact on how they behave with each other. If they feel loved and valued by us – rather than feeling judged and insecure – they are less likely to feel angry and lash out at their siblings. In this section we cover the issue of 'favourites', as well as comparisons and labels.

Favourites

Few parents admit to having a favourite child, even to themselves, and it's something that's rarely discussed. And yet having an obvious favourite will probably lead to more sibling rivalry and resentment than any other factor.

The reality, in most cases, is that we love our children with equal primal ferocity. But we have different relationships with each of our children, and our feelings for them change. Let's face it, we all favour our least irritating child, and this can change from one day to the next – or even hour by hour. Likewise, we tend to prefer an easy child to a difficult one. Again this can change – today's chuckling baby is tomorrow's Mummy-hitting 4-year-old.

It's important to keep a sense of perspective and to acknowledge that our feelings for our children are forever changing. If we feel favouritism towards one of our children, it probably won't last long. But we must take care that we don't become much closer to one of our children at the expense of another. And even more crucially, we must never let any of our children feel like the least favoured child. There are lots of steps you can take to prevent favouritism from becoming an issue.

What You Can Do

Reflect on why you find one of your children difficult, and take responsibility for your own feelings. Admit to yourself if you've 'gone off' one of your children. Try hard to build a relationship with this 'difficult' child by spending time alone with him to help strengthen your bond.

Be more tactile with your older children. We naturally have more physical contact with our younger children because they need more lifting, nappy-changing, help with shoes and so on. You can even this out by sitting your eldest on your knee for a story, or just stroking his head. Touch is a good way to restore your bond with your eldest. It is particularly useful after a tantrum, or if he has hurt your younger child and you've been feeling angry towards him.

Swap the script. For example, if you take the exact words you use to say goodnight to your youngest and repeat these to your eldest, you may be surprised at how gentle it sounds. Once you are aware of this difference, you can address it.

Accept that our children's needs change. If one of them is starting school, you're bound to 'favour' her for a few weeks as you give her extra time and attention, ensuring that she's happy and settled. Likewise, you'll 'favour' another of your children if he becomes ill. In an ideal world we'd give each of our children this special attention all the time.

Aim to make each of your children feel particularly special. Compliment them privately, using lots of descriptive praise. And show you appreciate their individuality by having activities that are unique to the two of you, such as a favourite book that you both love, a game or a silly messing-about ritual – anything that will make your children feel cherished for their individuality.

Comparisons

One of the wonderful things about having more than one child is how different they are. It's fascinating to watch them grow up into their own unique person. But how many of us unthinkingly make comparisons between our children, or label them?

It's easy to say: 'Your sister could put her shoes on by your age,' or, 'Your brother has eaten so nicely, why can't you?' This can be very crushing for children. It would be better to say, 'I think you're so grown-up that you may be able to put your shoes on by yourself today.' Or, 'You're really good at eating these days; yesterday you ate nearly everything.'

Even positive comparisons can be damaging. For example, if our youngest completes a jigsaw we may say, 'Wow you're clever, just like your sister.' The comparison diminishes the praise because we're not looking at the child as an individual. It would be better to say, 'Wow, that's clever – you completed that puzzle all by yourself.' Even if your youngest hero-worships her older sibling, being compared with him will probably make her feel uncomfortable.

Comparisons can sometimes make our children feel competitive and resentful towards each other because they are being judged and compared by Mum and Dad, and pitted against each other.

Labels

It's very easy to label our children – the clever one, the difficult one, the naughty one, the sensible one and so on. Negative labels obviously affect a child's self-esteem. Another problem is that siblings may start to use these labels to address their brother or sister. The labelled child soon starts to see themselves as 'difficult' or 'naughty', which can be extremely damaging.

Positive labels can also have a negative effect. We may think we're being encouraging and positive when we describe our children as the clever one, the artistic one or the musical one. But the label can become a habit and it puts pressure on children to be that label, and so it restricts them from being anything else. With siblings, if your brother or sister is labelled the 'clever one', where does that leave you? Probably feeling jealous, resentful and inferior.

Nicknames can have a similar negative effect – we may think we're being light-hearted and affectionate when we call our children, 'clever clogs', 'little-un' or 'boss', but these are still labels. It's much better to call them by their actual names.

Of course we need to encourage our children to do well, and sometimes push them a bit. But if we can do this without labelling them it will reduce unrealistic expectations, and putting pressure on them. Ideally we should aim to create a gentle atmosphere of acceptance in our homes. One way of doing this is to give children the message that we *can* be good at lots of things but we *can't* be good at everything. Making long lists of things that children are good at takes the pressure off for them to excel at one particular thing.

This attitude will help our children not to compare themselves to each other but to accept that they have different skills and are good at all sorts of things. It will also build their confidence and banish feelings of inferiority in the family. This not only helps younger children cope with the fact that their siblings have an age advantage, but also helps older children cope when their younger siblings show more natural skill at something than them.

Helping children to feel less inferior and competitive, especially in their parents' eyes, will help them not to fight each other quite as much.

HELP YOUR CHILDREN TO FEEL LESS JEALOUS AND ANGRY

Having a baby brother or sister can fill small children with extreme emotions. One minute they will be filled with love, smothering their sibling with kisses; the next they'll feel suddenly angry and squeeze the baby so tightly that she cries.

Extreme, fast-changing emotions are entirely normal, which is why you should never leave a new baby alone with an older sibling, especially if the older one is 4 or younger. After this age they are unlikely to lash out at their siblings quite so randomly, but will do so when there's a reason, even if it's a very minor reason.

Helping our children to release their anger and jealousy – or, better still, helping them not to get angry in the first place – will make them less likely to lash out at their siblings. Here's how:

Allow Your Children to Talk about Hating their Siblings

When they say they hate each other – and they will, and they'll probably wish each other dead from time to time, too – the worst thing you can say is, 'You can't say that.' This will frustrate them and force them to repress their feelings, which, in a worst-case scenario, can result in years of built-up resentment. Give them a let-out by listening and then saying, 'Yes, it must be hard for you having a brother/sister.'

Point Out the Good Things about Siblings

When your children do happen to get along, highlight this and use it to 'sell' the idea that having siblings is a positive thing. For example, 'You've got such a funny sister; she makes life more fun, doesn't she? And she's lucky to have a big brother like you because you've got so many fun ideas and you can make her laugh.' Flattering your children can help them to be more open-minded to the benefits of having siblings. You can also explain that some children don't have a brother or sister to play with.

Who's the Cutest?

As children approach 2 they learn to entertain the family and make everyone laugh. This can be incredibly cute, but also rather unsettling for older children who may copy the performance but get only a lukewarm response. They can end up feeling over-sized and unappealing, then become jealous of their sibling. We've found that it helps if you turn the attention to the older child and give them praise for having such a funny brother or sister – for example, 'You've got such a funny sister, she must have learned it from you.'

Handle Tale-telling with Care

Telling tales starts in earnest from the age of about 4 and, depending on your reaction, it can make children extremely angry. The culprit will feel victimized and ganged-up on by you and his sibling, and he'll become bitterly resentful towards his sibling. But we're not going to suggest that you ban tale-telling, because in a busy household it can be extremely useful. For example, if one of your children is hanging out of an upstairs window, you'll want to know about it.

What we do say is handle the tale-telling with care, or it will not only become an extremely annoying habit but will damage the relationship between your children. The reason children tell tales is usually because it gets them attention and also makes them feel powerful watching another child get into trouble. So we advise that when your child tells a tale, avoid punishing the 'naughty' child and don't over-praise the tell-tale – a simple 'Thanks for letting me know what's going on' will do. She won't become a regular tell-tale because the reward simply isn't great enough.

Sometimes she'll tell you that her sibling has hurt her – cuddle and comfort her and say that her brother/sister shouldn't hurt her. Then have a quiet word with the culprit later, if possible when the 'tell-tale' isn't around. This deals with the situation but doesn't add fuel to it by giving the tell-tale gloating power, and so making the culprit feel over-resentful and even less likely to be 'nice' next time.

Be Understanding if They Steal

If a child under the age of about 8 steals, it's almost certainly because he's feeling angry but powerless. Perhaps he's fed up with being hurt by an older sibling – he hasn't got the strength to retaliate physically, so instead he takes his sibling's toys and stashes them under his bed as a way of getting back. Or maybe he feels unfairly told off for hurting a younger sibling, so he steals and hides her toys when he feels really angry with her. Or he may even take your things (phone or keys, for example) because he's furious with you. There's little point in punishing a young child's stealing – it's unlikely to prevent it. It's much better to get to the root of the problem, because if you can help your child feel less angry and powerless he'll probably stop stealing.

Listen to Their Excuses

When your eldest attacks your youngest, you may well be so furious that you banish the attacker to his room, telling him you're not interested in his excuses. But what you're failing to acknowledge is that your youngest may well have become a master at winding up her older sibling – children learn to tease from as early as 18 months, for instance by grabbing a toy in order to provoke another child. Your eldest would almost certainly have been provoked and will be feeling even more hostile towards the younger child by your refusal to listen to him. By allowing him to have his say, you can help him release some of his frustration and feel slightly less angry towards his sibling. You can also say to him, 'Even if someone annoys us, we don't hurt; we tell an adult.' It's also important to address the cause of the problem – the annoying younger sibling.

Race the Clock, Not Each Other

When you've got more than one child, it's very tempting to set up races to speed everyone up a bit – for example getting dressed in the morning, or the first one upstairs to the bathroom. But your children will become pumped full of adrenaline and be extremely competitive – there will almost certainly be gloating and tears at the end of the race. So everything actually takes longer than usual, because you've got to spend time calming the 'loser'. It's much better to get everyone to race the clock – 3 minutes to get dressed, for example. When they start shouting 'I won!' you can say, 'We're racing the clock not each other.' Then everyone's a winner and there's less gloating.

This technique works equally well during play, such as puzzle-making competitions, or running races – if children are racing a stopwatch, it's less fraught than racing each other, but still lots of fun. And the loser will find it easier to cope with not getting such a good 'time' than if their sibling races past them screaming, 'I've won!'

Presents, Clothes and Shoes

Plenty of families end up in a situation where they can't buy one child a new coat without buying a coat for the other kids, too. Or parents buy identical toys to prevent fights. Before the age of about 4, children don't have the capacity to be calculating, so are blissfully unaware if someone else is being given more than them. But from 4 a child may complain if a sibling is given a bigger present than them, or a greater number of presents. From the age of about 6, children are capable of assessing the value of presents, and as they approach 7 they may start to obsess about who's being given what, and can become very angry if they think it's not fair.

You can avoid this by making Christmas and birthdays reasonably fair – and why wouldn't you? And there's no need to give non-birthday children a present, just explain that everyone benefits when there's a birthday because there's cake to eat and new toys to share (on the birthday-child's terms, of course).

When it comes to clothes and shoes, point out that it all balances out and give the jealous child plenty of examples – you needed shoes last week but your brother didn't because his feet hadn't grown, and we bought you a coat in the winter because yours wasn't warm enough, and so on.

If you're being fair overall, your children will realize this especially if you take the time to point it out to them. And if they keep going on about something being unfair, listen to them – perhaps they have a point. If they are being reasonable you can address it, and if they are being unreasonable you can dismiss it – with a clear explanation as to why.

WHY SIBLINGS FIGHT

Even if you tackle favouritism and take steps to help your children feel less angry, disagreements will still happen. As we've said before, sibling rivalry is not something you can solve, just something you learn to manage. Here we talk about some of the reasons children fight, and what you can do about it.

Tiredness or Hunger

Being hungry or tired are known to make us irritable, so keep a particularly close watch over your children when you know this to be the case. Before the age of 3 children are particularly affected by hunger or tiredness. This gradually lessens with age, but never goes away completely.

Boredom

Sometimes children jump on each other or attack simply because they are bored. Ensure your children have plenty to do. It takes less time and energy to set up paints and clear them away later than to deal with persistent bickering and fighting.

They Have Nothing to Lose

It is thought that one of the reasons siblings lash out at each other far more frequently and viciously than at their friends is that there is less to lose. If you treat a friend badly there will be repercussions – children as young as 3 say, 'I'm not your friend anymore,' and by 4 they say it with meaning. Your brother or sister will always be there.

However, if siblings can have fun laughing, joking and playing together, there will be more to lose when they fall out. A child won't want to play with her sibling if he's just punched her. Or if siblings are playing hide and seek and one of them persists in bickering, the other child will eventually refuse to play at all. If they usually have fun together, this will be more of a loss. So spending time messing about and playing with both your children and showing them how much fun they can have together will teach them how much there is to lose when they fight.

They're Feeling Ignored

In the real world we argue with our partner, and we have to cope with illness, bereavement and losing our jobs. And often we have to take work phone calls, or just feel tired and fed up. During these times we are likely to overlook our children, who may well discover that bashing their sibling is the most effective way to get their parents' attention, and has the added benefit of releasing anger. These are the times that most of us resort to television and computer games – but these props will only do so much. Children always need parental attention. So, however hard it seems, reading a story to your children or playing a board game is definitely easier than sorting out constant fighting, which you'll find particularly miserable when you're feeling down or stressed.

COPING STRATEGIES FOR WHEN THEY FIGHT

The sickening feeling when a fight breaks out between your children is probably one of the worst things about parenting. As you race towards the thumps and screams you have a knot of dread in your stomach. Thankfully, in most cases the noise is far worse than the damage, and siblings rarely do each other serious harm. It's almost unheard of for siblings to end up in hospital as a result of fighting each other.

In fact there are even some benefits to sibling fighting – it teaches negotiation skills, assertiveness, compromise and self-control, and is good preparation for the playground because children learn to stand up for themselves. It also helps teach forgiveness and how to say sorry.

Sibling rivalry is still something that parents have to deal with, and it's not easy. It's particularly hard going in the early years. A baby can start to bite in anger from about 16 months, and will have the physical capacity to fight back hard by around 2 years of age. And violence peaks between 3 and 5 years – children of this age are estimated to have around four squabbles and fights an hour. Of course, sibling disputes don't stop here – it continues well into adolescence and beyond.

So how should we respond? When our children fight it's easy to get very emotional, which can sometimes make things worse. This is why it's important to plan our response beforehand, as this can help us stay calm and rational, and therefore teach our children to get along better. Here is a selection of strategies for various types of fight.

DON'T LET THEM FIGHT IT OUT

Letting them just fight it out can be very tempting, especially if your children have been squabbling most of the day and you're exhausted and fed up with rushing to separate them. But ignoring a fight can mean that younger children end up feeling abandoned and let down by parents, and older children can start to bully.

There are exceptions – see low-grade bickering (page 163) and play-fighting (page 170). But even in these cases we suggest that you still remain alert, because innocuous arguing or play-fighting can easily turn into an angry punch-up.

Low-grade Bickering

This is incredibly common and can sometimes be the starting point for a more serious fight. If there is no violence or nasty teasing and neither child is becoming upset, this is one of the few exceptions where you can let them 'fight it out'. Some children like to bicker almost for the sake of it, and it is certainly good for developing verbal reasoning and arguing skills. Keep listening in case it gets nasty – bickering can turn to violence within seconds (see pages 164–66 for how to handle aggressive fights).

As children get older they start to have slanging matches, which can get abusive and spiteful. Paying a small fine every time anyone in the family swears or uses nasty names ('poo-poo head' obviously doesn't count) is a quick way to put a stop to this. Your children can help to decide which terms of abuse are unacceptable and warrant a fine.

Teasing

Older children may verbally tease their baby sibling if, for example, she doesn't say 'banana' properly. Or perhaps they'll ask her, 'Are you a poo poo?' and she'll reply 'Yes,' which can be highly amusing for a 6-year-old. Until the age of about 3 your baby won't mind in the slightest, and will relish the attention from the older sibling she idolizes but who is often not especially interested in her. So our advice is not to tell your eldest off or teasing could become an attention-seeking device.

Once your youngest reaches 3 and objects to being teased, you'll need to intervene. Do bear in mind that the more fuss you and your youngest make about the teasing, the more your eldest will do it. On the other hand, he'll soon tire of teasing if it's not having the desired effect of upsetting everyone.

Of course you must explain that it's wrong to upset people. But it's actually more effective to spend time teaching your youngest not to react. You can try asking her if her older brother/sister teases the chair, with the answer being 'No,' of course, 'because teasing a chair is no fun as it doesn't react.' Likewise, her older brother/sister doesn't tease Mum or Dad, because Mum and Dad don't mind teasing, so it's no fun.

It takes a while, but as your youngest learns not to react so strongly, the teasing eases. What's more, using this method gives lots of attention to the child being teased and pretty much ignores the perpetrator.

Bullying – When One Child is Being Far More Aggressive than the Other

This can occur as a result of a minor squabble escalating out of control, or when a child is retaliating because they are particularly livid. The aggressor, usually the older child, can do a lot of physical harm – you're likely to see bleeding scratch marks and bruising after such a fight. The victim will not only be hurt but feel frightened and let down by parents if they don't come to her rescue.

This is the most vicious and upsetting of all sibling fights, and it's the most likely to make you lose the plot. Don't. It's also essential that you don't take sides – not easy, but here's how.

As soon as you hear such a fight and are rushing to help, call out to your youngest that you are coming to help. As well as giving your youngest some comfort, it may be enough to make the perpetrator back off, although he's usually so enraged that he won't hear you. When you reach the fight scene, pull your eldest away from your youngest – you can try tickling him to make him release his grip, and if this doesn't work, yank him away hard – there's no politically correct way of doing this.

Send him immediately to his room, telling him that you'll listen to his side of the story later. Putting the attacker in another room is the quickest way of taking the heat out of the situation.

Take your youngest in your arms and comfort her. Sometimes after a particularly hard pummelling, a child may not want to tell you what happened. This can be frustrating because you're trying to assess if she is badly hurt (it's unlikely to be more serious than scratching and bruising).

You'll also be desperate for information, as you'll be shocked as to how your own children can be this aggressive. But the victim can feel so stressed and upset that talking is too much effort. So allow her to recover in her own time before she talks.

Children don't have the developmental capacity to conceal the truth until at least 3½, so will tell you exactly what happened during a fight – for example, 'I hit him then he kicked me back, then he punched me.' This obviously makes it easier for you to get to the bottom of what happened. And always use this to set an example to your older child about the importance of owning up – 'Own up and I'll be less cross' is a very useful message to instil in your family.

With an older child it may take more time to find out what happened. She almost certainly annoyed her older sibling, and it's helpful if you can gently persuade her to admit this. When she does, you can explain why her older sibling became angry – although do spell out that he was wrong to hurt her.

Then you can give her a strategy to stop the same thing from happening again. For example, try not to make him cross by playing with his new Lego toy because it can break easily. If he hurts you then say, 'Stop hurting me.' If he doesn't stop, shout 'Help' so that Mum or Dad can intervene quickly.

Once you've comforted your youngest, talk to your eldest. By this time you'll be feeling calmer, and so will your eldest. If you can begin by telling him that his sibling has admitted to annoying him by breaking his Lego, he'll be far more receptive to listening to you telling him that 'We don't hurt.' Listen to his side of the story and sympathize, as this will help him not to hate his sibling quite so much (as we explain on page 158, 'Listen to Their Excuses').

Unless this is an exceptional one-off, you'll need to punish your eldest child – for example, no television or computers for a day. Don't make his punishment too big (no TV for a week, for example) because you probably won't carry it out, and also your child will feel despondent and feel like 'giving up' rather than wanting to start afresh the next day. Explain to your child that you're punishing him because he lost his temper and hurt his sibling. Eventually he'll learn to control his violent rage, because he knows there's a consequence – it may take a while.

And from the age of about 5 he'll understand the following: 'I can see that your younger sister annoys you, but as soon as you hurt her you are in the wrong. So I have to tell you off and not her. Next time tell me if she annoys you, then I can stop her and you won't be in trouble.'

Don't punish him by 'rewarding' the victim – for example giving her something nice to eat, or snuggling down to watch a film together while he's banished from watching television. This will just make him feel more hostile than ever towards her. There's also a chance that it will encourage the victim to provoke her sibling next time – or at least not discourage her too much.

The ideal solution is to prevent such a fight happening in the first place. But the reality is that sibling fights tend to break out in seconds, and if we don't happen to be at the scene, we're left to just cope with the aftermath.

SAYING SORRY

Don't force an apology after such an aggressive fight, as this could make your children feel more hostile towards each other. What you can do is wait a few hours until feelings have calmed, then ask the aggressor if he feels sorry. If he says no, leave it. If he says yes, then suggest he apologizes to his sibling. Likewise, you can gently suggest that the child who was hurt apologizes for winding up her sibling.

A genuine apology can be quite cathartic for children, but it's unrealistic to expect it after every fight and squabble. Encourage saying sorry, by all means, but try to accept it if your children are reluctant. It's more important to gently build their relationship than to drive home moral values.

An Evenly Matched Fight

Both your children will be attacking each other in this fight. Unlike with bullying, there won't be a frightened victim or an aggressor attacking with out-of-control abandon as we describe on pages 164–66. Again, it will probably start as a squabble and then escalate.

As with the bullying fight, it's important to step in quickly and to physically separate your children. But you won't need to send one of them away, because they won't be quite as livid as with a bullying fight.

Instead, they'll be desperate to tell you it was the other one's fault, and will inevitably be shouting at the top of their voices. Tell them you can only listen to one at a time, then, as soon as you can, summarize in a few words what each child is trying to tell you. Once they realize that you seem to understand their point of view, they will start to calm down and, with luck, stop shouting.

Then you need to listen to each story, unpicking the facts and working out how it started. You'll need to be razor-sharp and very speedy, as your children will find listening to their sibling's side of events intolerable. As soon as you've got a clear understanding of events, you can summarize and your children will feel calm. And if you can possibly bring humour into your summary, they will feel calmer still (you'll have to judge this carefully, of course, or they may think you are teasing them).

An example of such a fight may be if a child is watching television and the other one switches channel mid-programme. The watcher gets annoyed and tries to grab the remote control – there's a tussle, and a fight breaks out. The television-watcher uses the remote control as a weapon and all hell breaks loose. This all takes place in about 20 seconds, so even if you race to the scene you won't get there quickly enough to stop a fight in the first place, but you will be able to break it up and start the 'inquest'.

Once you've unravelled the situation it can be useful to bring in humour to help teach your children not to fight next time. For instance, 'Daddy finds some of my programmes very boring and I'd be extremely annoyed if he marched in and switched channels. But I wouldn't hit him over the head with the remote control.'

Imagining adults re-enacting a sibling fight can be very amusing for children, and it can also help them to understand how unacceptable their behaviour is. It is at this point that they will be open to suggestions as to how to handle a similar situation better next time. For example, 'We don't switch channels when someone else is watching. And, if someone annoys us we don't hurt them, we tell them to stop and if they don't, we tell an adult.'

Always suggest that both children apologize after a fight but, as we've said previously, don't force it. If a younger child is keen to kiss an older child sorry, you can suggest she 'kisses his soft hair' – this will be more acceptable to her older sibling than if she gave him a wet, slobbery kiss on his face. Before the age of 2, children will happily kiss and hug their siblings, but this gradually changes as they become aware of 'germs'. By the time they reach about 4, children can start to feel physically repelled by their siblings and may not want to be affectionate towards them.

Squabbling Over a Toy

This is one of the most common reasons siblings fall out, and it can begin from as young as 18 months, when babies become possessive and determined to grab hold of another child's toy. Until your youngest reaches 2½ and is developmentally capable of understanding the concept of sharing, we suggest you take the path of least resistance. So if your baby can be fobbed off with an alternative toy, or distracted, do it. Likewise, if you can appeal to an older child's sense of reason and persuade him to give the baby the toy to prevent a tantrum, do it. And babies will sometimes give a toy to an older sibling if he 'asks nicely' – always worth a try.

Then, as your youngest approaches 2½, you can gradually introduce sharing and taking turns. There are dozens of variations, but one method that works is letting one child play with a toy for 5 more minutes, then it's someone else's turn.

If children are fighting over different pieces, for example building blocks, you can put all the blocks in the middle then let them take turns choosing a block that they 'need' until the blocks are divided up evenly. Next time you could try persuading them to build as a team, sharing all the blocks.

You may have to consider who the toy belongs to, then give the owner a privilege. For example, he could be the one to choose a building block first. Or he could have first turn playing with something – unless, of course, his sibling was playing with the toy first. It's a minefield and, frankly, it doesn't matter too much how you make things fair in your family, just try to be consistent.

You will teach the sharing lesson hundreds of times, and sometimes it will seem as though your children will never learn. But persevere, because over the months, and even years, they *will* learn. And the proof is that children with siblings nearly always find it easier to share than children without. Hardly surprising, seeing as they've had hundreds of lessons on the subject.

As children get older (around 6½) you can encourage them to work out their own property disputes. Flatter them by saying you're sure they'll find a fair solution, then leave them to it.

Some parents settle a dispute by removing the toy being fought over. Although this makes the parent feel as though they are taking control, it leaves the children feeling angry and doesn't teach them to share. If you're having one of those days when you're about to explode and the only solution seems to be taking the toy away, then try saying, 'I'll put it up here for now to keep it safe.' This will help calm your children, as they will feel relieved that their sibling isn't getting it, they'll be able to see it, and will assume they will get to play with it later.

Play-fighting

This is particularly common between brothers. And parents of two or more testosterone-driven boys will be very familiar with the constant wrestling and rolling around on the floor which, incidentally, continues until adolescence. But it's a very good release for their aggression.

During a play-fight you'll see lots of pushing, shoving, pinning-down and grabbing, as well as lots of smiling and laughing. If you watch carefully, you'll also see that your eldest (biggest) child will often put himself in a weaker position, allowing the younger sibling to make a counter-attack. This is called self-handicapping. You'll see the role of the attacker and defender swap constantly during a play-fight. This never happens in a real fight. The other big difference is that no one gets hurt, unless it's an accident, and then the opponent will show lots of concern.

If someone gets hurt during a play-fight, and of course this happens, the culprit will be very willing to apologize – if he's not, it suggests that the fight wasn't quite so 'playful' after all. Assuming it was just a play-fight that went wrong, comfort the smaller child and explain that the bigger one wasn't trying to hurt her. Talk through what happened with both your children, and work out together how they will do things differently next time – for example that the little one calls 'time-out' sooner, they choose a softer surface to fight on, or the bigger one watches the little one's face to check that she's still happy and not getting angry.

Play-fighting is generally not allowed in nurseries or schools, so do allow it in your home because there are so many benefits.

First, it's exhausting so will tire out your children, leaving them feeling calmer and less aggressive. It's also good for muscle development and gross motor skills. And it's good for impulse control, because during a play-fight you've got to hold back enough not to hurt your opponent.

There's no need to intervene during a play-fight. You can ask, 'Is this a play-fight or real?' just to reassure yourself before you leave them to it. And you can insist on no head-locks, punching (pushing is OK, but no fists), or shoes (children are far less likely to get hurt accidently if they aren't wearing shoes).

You can teach your children a 'time-out' rule. One of them shouts 'time-out' when it's all getting too rough, then the other child has to stop immediately. This is good for self-control. It also teaches children that they have the power to get out of a situation they don't like – one day this may give them the confidence to stand up to bullies.

CHAPTER 12
Illness and Injury

When you've got two children, it's tougher than ever when one of them is ill. As well as looking after your sick child you also have to think about your other child, who will almost certainly get a bit jealous and be more demanding.

Other things to consider are whether your healthy child will become infected and, if they aren't at school yet, coping with them becoming bored and misbehaving at the doctor's surgery, the pharmacist, and even A&E. On top of all this you'll have to contend with the inevitable broken nights and perhaps getting ill yourself.

On the plus side, as a second-time mum you'll be more astute when it comes to recognizing when your children are only mildly ill and so don't need a doctor – fewer trips to the GP's surgery can be a blessing when you've got two children in tow. Having said that, always see your doctor if you are concerned about one of your children – you'll find that your doctor takes you particularly seriously now that you are a second-time mum because it generally takes quite a lot to worry a mum of two. And, as always, it's better to be reassured that there's nothing wrong than for your child to miss out on medical care.

COPING WHEN EVERYONE IS ILL

When one of your children has an infectious illness, it's very common for the rest of the family, particularly other children, to catch it. Of course you can take precautions such as frequent hand-washing to help prevent the spread of stomach bugs and the common cold virus, but there's no point in becoming too obsessed. In fact, it's often seen as an advantage – if for example chickenpox is spread to a sibling, it gets it out of the way and also means they won't be off school, as they may have been had they caught it when they were older.

Likewise with colds. There are about 100 common cold viruses and each time we catch one, our body builds up its immunity against a specific virus so we won't catch that particular strain again. So second and subsequent children catch lots more colds when they are babies but are relatively healthy later on, and miss less school. It also explains why by the time we are elderly, we rarely catch colds.

But just because there is a biological advantage to your children spreading their germs, this doesn't make it any easier to cope on a practical level. Our advice is to go into survival mode, especially if you too are ill – so TV, snacks, infant ibuprofen, Calpol, treats and bribes. Forget about your usual standards, this is only temporary. The following survival tips may help:

- Diarrhoea – put older children in nappies or pull-ups if they will tolerate it – much easier than washing clothes and sheets.

- Vomiting – put a large towel over the pillow and top end of the bed, as this makes cleaning up much easier. Put cuddly toys at the end of the bed.

- Put your children to bed at their usual time or earlier – ill children tend to go to sleep quite easily.

- Don't waste time trying to get a sick child to eat. Just ensure they have plenty to drink. You could also dig out your old baby bottles – a bottle of warm milk will comfort some children even if they are about 5! This is useful if they are off their food, but don't let this become a habit as there is a link between obesity and drinking from bottles after the age of 2.

• Liquid antibiotics for children aren't always palatable despite their lemon or strawberry flavours. A chocolate button after each spoonful usually does the trick.

WHEN YOU CAN TAKE YOUR CHILD TO SEE YOUR PHARMACIST RATHER THAN YOUR GP

It's far more convenient to see your pharmacist than your GP for certain ailments, as you don't need to book or queue. The only disadvantages are that without a prescription you won't get your child's treatment for free, and you won't be able to get any prescription-only medicines. But your pharmacist will be able to tell you if you need to take your child to the GP, or indeed to A&E.

If your child has a rash but no fever, your pharmacist will almost certainly be able to help, and be able to diagnose common skin conditions such as impetigo, ringworm and dermatitis. He can also help you diagnose chickenpox – very useful in the early stages when you may not be sure if your child has it.

With ringworm, dermatitis and chickenpox, you'll be able to buy a cream and go home. But with impetigo you'll need to see your GP to get a prescription for an antibiotic cream.

WHEN YOU CAN TELEPHONE YOUR DOCTOR RATHER THAN VISIT

Some GP surgeries are happy to speak to patients over the phone to help you decide whether you need to book a face-to-face appointment with the doctor.

This is perfect for those occasions when you're a little bit worried about your child but don't think you need to see the doctor just yet.

You can also phone NHS direct 24 hours a day – 0845 4647. (Please note that from April 2013 there are plans for this number to be replaced by the phone number 111.)

WHEN YOU NEED TO VISIT YOUR GP

If you know what's wrong with your child, for example she has chickenpox or a tummy bug, then you can probably manage her illness at home. But if you have no idea what's wrong with your child and yet she has a fever between 38.5°C and 40°C, or seems unwell, then take her to your GP.

With babies under 3 months, take them to the GP if they have a fever between 37.5°C and 38.4°C. Young babies with fevers higher than this need to go to A&E – see page 178.

PROTECTING YOUR BABY FROM INFECTION

Babies under 6 months have natural immunity to chickenpox from their mothers. You can reduce the chances of your baby catching a cold by stopping infected siblings touching her hands – the cold virus is transferred from nose mucus to someone else's eyes or nose. If your older child has a stomach bug, it's particularly important that they don't touch the baby for a few days as diarrhoea and sickness in babies can be dangerous because of the dehydration risk. And everyone else must wash their hands before touching the baby.

GO TO A&E OR WAIT IT OUT?

Going to hospital with two children is something none of us wants to do, and sometimes you may not know if an injury or illness is serious enough for a visit. For example, if your toddler splits his lip at bathtime – there's blood everywhere, but do you really need to get everyone dressed again, then load them into the car and take them to hospital?

Thankfully, in this particular instance you almost certainly don't need to go to A&E – lips bleed a lot, and heal quickly. Just ensure that the bleeding stops within 10 minutes and in the meantime put pressure on the cut using a clean cloth and perhaps a bag of frozen peas to help soothe it. You also need to check that the cut doesn't cross the 'vermilion border' – the line around your lips where you would draw your lip liner. Cuts over this line don't heal easily and need stitches.

The following information may help you to make a decision as to whether you need to go to hospital. But *always* go if you are worried – now that you've got two children, you're unlikely to be fussing unnecessarily. If it does turn out to be a false alarm, no one at the hospital will mind in the slightest. And don't hesitate about going back again later if you are still worried.

Fever

If your child has a temperature of 40°C or higher even after she's had Calpol or infant ibuprofen, you need to take her to A&E. Likewise if your baby is under 3 months and has a temperature of 38.5°C or higher, you need to take her to A&E. This is because very young babies have poor immune function, and standard practice is to treat them in hospital if they have a fever.

Falls

If your child is still upset after 2 hours, she may have broken a bone. Green stick fractures are particularly common in young children because their bones are soft and bendy – these incomplete breaks to the bone don't usually show any deformity so can only be detected with an x-ray (take her to A&E). Your child may hold her arm to protect it, or be unable to walk, and she will probably be unusually quiet and look pale. She'll also cry out if you accidently move her limb – for example while getting her out of the car.

Bumps to the Head

Children are forever bumping their heads, and you obviously don't take them to hospital each time. Always take your child to A&E if he loses consciousness, or is floppy, drowsy or feeling sick after bumping his head. Or if he bashes his temple – the soft part of the head with no protective skull bone.

If this isn't the case but you are still worried, you have a choice of either taking your child straight to hospital, where he will hopefully be given the all clear, or you could call your GP, who may be able to reassure you over the phone or may see your child as an emergency patient. Depending on where the bruise is and the severity, your GP will either reassure you or send you along to A&E.

Cuts

If it's not bleeding too much after about 10 minutes, it is probably OK. But if it looks deep and you think it may need stitches, you could pop in to see your pharmacist. He will either advise you to go to A&E or perhaps sell you a dressing or sterilized strips to stop the wound(s) from re-opening.

IF YOU DO HAVE TO GO TO A&E

Having to wait for several hours in A&E on your own is tedious enough, but doing this with one or more children can be miserable. Here are some tips for getting through it:

- Grab snacks and drinks if you can – even if the hospital café is open, you won't dare pop out because you never know when you will be called.

- Take your child's comfort toy if possible.

- There will probably be toys to play with at the hospital. Be prepared to get on the floor and play with your child even if it's 2 a.m. Even children with broken bones will happily play with toys in a hospital waiting room, and will find the act of playing extremely comforting.

- Explain to your child what is going on at each stage, however young she is. And do explain everything to your other child if he is with you as he too will be feeling anxious, and also rather left out. He may well express his anxiety by playing up, which will make him seem uncaring – he does care, he's just stressed and also bored. Try to give him some positive attention, however stressed or tired you're feeling – it will help to calm him and make your life easier.

- If you are able to leave your healthy child at home, perhaps with Dad, do ensure that he understands where you and his brother or sister are going. He'll be worried even if he doesn't show it.

CALLING AN AMBULANCE

If you need an ambulance, for example if your child loses consciousness, only one parent will be allowed to accompany your child. But if you are on your own you'll be allowed to bring any other children in the ambulance with you.

SIBLING JEALOUSY WHEN THE OTHER CHILD IS ILL

Children can become more demanding and jealous than usual when their sibling is unwell. This is because they see their sick brother or sister getting extra attention from Mum and Dad, and perhaps the doctor, too. At the doctor's surgery you can give your healthy child a treat for being patient – a sticker will usually do.

So, as well as looking after your sick child, you'll also have to give your healthy child extra fuss. You can take her temperature from time to time and ask how she is feeling, just as you are no doubt doing with your sick child. And do allow for her being more bad-tempered than usual, as she may well be coming down with the same bug, or perhaps getting over it and still feeling a bit unwell.

You can also give your healthy child a spoonful of liquid vitamin drops when she sees you giving your sick child medicine – take care not to give more than the stated dose. Giving 'medicine' is particularly helpful for jealous toddlers, who perceive not getting medicine as traumatic as if you were giving sweets to their sibling but leaving them out. Likewise, your child may insist on 'sharing' his sibling's asthma inhaler – an occasional puff of the blue preventer inhaler (ventolin) won't do him any harm.

Your healthy child will want to stay off school, just like her sick sibling. Sell the idea that it's better to be well than sick. Explain that by going to school she won't be missing any fun at home, because children who are ill go to bed while Mum gets on with the laundry and checking emails. After school tell your child how much her sick brother or sister slept during the day (sleeping will sound incredibly dull to a child), and also how they were so ill they didn't even want to eat yummy things (say a chocolate biscuit), so she can eat it instead. And do point out the upside of having a sick sibling – more treats for everyone else.

Encourage her to help look after her sick sibling – children love doing this, even if they are vile to their siblings the rest of the time.

Make it a rule that children are allowed to stay off school if they have a temperature of 38°C or more. This is will minimize jealousy and accusations of 'It's not fair', because body temperature is an objective measurement – and so it's the thermometer making the decision, not Mum favouring one of her children. If your well child knows that as soon as her temperature goes up she too will stay off school, she'll feel much better about the situation. And from the age of about 6 she may well take her own temperature, especially if you have an ear thermometer which is easy to use and read.

GIVE CALPOL AND INFANT IBUPROFEN FREELY

Don't hold back on giving your children infant paracetamol (Calpol) or infant ibuprofen – but always stick to the doses stated on the pack, of course. And remember that your children may need different doses, depending on their ages. If your child is big for his age you can check the dosage with your pharmacist, as you may be able to give him more.

The correct dose of children's ibuprofen will have no effect on your child's stomach – children have very resilient stomach linings. And children's paracetamol won't damage your child's liver, because young children metabolize this drug more efficiently than adults. Infant drugs are very safe, and most paediatricians happily give them to their own children very freely – sticking to the recommended doses, of course.

Giving these drugs to your child round the clock will keep her fever down and also make her feel more comfortable. Do write down what you give your children, because it's easy to forget and give them too much, especially if you too are ill. And communicate with your partner – if he's the one getting up in the night, he'll need to know how much medicine a child has had and at what time she can have another dose.

Using both infant paracetamol and ibuprofen means that you can give your child more painkillers, as these drugs work in different ways. So even if you've given the maximum amount of paracetamol, it is still safe to give your child ibuprofen. In fact, combining these drugs gives a super-powerful but safe painkilling effect, as ibuprofen and paracetamol work in synergy (multiplication rather than an additional effect). Combining these drugs is a good option before bedtime to help your child get a good night's sleep.

If you're just using one of these medications, we recommend ibuprofen. We've found this to be more effective than paracetamol, and it has a longer half-life, meaning its painkilling effects last longer so you don't have to give it as often.

Plan and time medicine doses so that your children have medicine just before bedtime. This means you'll hopefully only have to get up once in the night to give them another dose. You can also time medicine to be given before mealtimes, to encourage your child's appetite – he may feel better if he's able to eat something, but never force this.

ACCIDENTS

Once you have two children you may dread taking them to the park or the woods because it's so difficult to keep watch over your eldest while looking after a baby. As your children get older it becomes more challenging as they run off in different directions. And yet children are 25 times more likely to be injured in the home than in a playground, according to The Royal Society for the Prevention of Accidents (ROSPA).

Accidents in parks do happen, of course, with swings accounting for 41 per cent of all playground injuries, followed by climbing frames with 23 per cent, and slides with 21 per cent. But according to ROSPA, this doesn't mean that swings are dangerous, just very popular, as you find them in just about every children's playground. The only playground activity ROSPA warns as being dangerous is using the overhead bars that rotate.

A common reason for playground accidents is broken equipment, so do check it. Accidents can also occur if your child is competing and showing off, or just playing with older kids and so pushing herself beyond her ability.

But the chances of an accident are minimal and it's important to stand back and allow children to learn from having bumps and falls. Taking risks is an essential part of childhood development and learning. For example, you can tell a child not to cycle over an icy puddle in the park, but it's not until they try it, skid and perhaps fall off that they will fully understand the consequences. And this lesson could one day save their lives if they are ever out cycling, or indeed driving, on an icy road.

Giving your children freedom isn't easy – and mums tend to find this harder than dads! Although nearly three times as many children end up in hospital having fallen out of bed than falling out of a tree, according to NHS statistics, watching your child at the top of a tree can still make you feel sick with dread. But once you've got more than one child to look after, you'll actually be forced to give your eldest more freedom, which is great. Just be sure to give your youngest that same freedom when the time comes.

We've said that the home is far more risky for children than being out. So if an accident is going to happen, chances are it will be at home, particularly now that you've got two children. As well as the usual risks of scalds and falling down the stairs or out of windows, you've also got the potential risk of your older child accidently harming your youngest. For example, big kids love picking up small kids, which can lead to head injuries. They often pull smaller kids up by their wrists, which can lead to a pulled elbow when the elbow comes out of the socket. This is very common, and if it happens your child needs to go to hospital to have her elbow relocated. And older toddlers like to 'feed' babies with small toys, which can be a choking hazard.

Accidents often occur because it's impossible to watch both children at once – it's much harder to be vigilant when you've got more than one child. Our big tip is to be especially watchful when your children are together, as they are probably more likely to come to harm than when they are on their own. We've also found that once a child reaches 2 he doesn't need to be watched quite so closely – you can be downstairs, he can be upstairs and he'll probably be safe for a little while. A child younger than this will be at more risk and shouldn't be left alone.

And, of course, silence isn't always a good sign, especially if your children are together. Do keep checking to see what your children are up to, and don't be lulled by an unusually quiet period. As you may well have discovered, it often spells trouble. So however many precautions you've taken to make your home safe, don't become distracted from what your children are up to, as most kids are ingenious at discovering new dangers. And keep adapting your home as your children get older. For example, lots of children can open child-proof bottles by the age of about 4, so you'll need to lock these away.

CAR TRAVEL

Having two or more children means you're more likely to 'forget' to fasten their car seats. As you bundle them into the car it's all too easy to assume that your partner has strapped the children in – while he assumes you have. It's only when you arrive at your destination that you realize, with a horrible sick feeling, that one or more of the children wasn't strapped in. So work out a checking system to ensure that each child gets strapped in for every journey.

Having two or more children also makes it harder to watch both of them. But it's essential to check that no one is standing or playing behind a car that's being reversed out of a drive or parking spot. A driver won't see a toddler because of his/her blind spot. Tragically, young children have been injured or killed when the family car has been reversed into them.

FIRE

Fit smoke alarms, as children are far more vulnerable to smoke inhalation than adults. And talk to your children about what to do if there is a fire – small children instinctively hide from danger and the time spent finding them can be fatal. According to Childalert (www.childalert.co.uk), 46 per cent of fatal accidents to children are caused by fire.

WHEN YOU DON'T REALIZE ONE OF YOUR CHILDREN IS ILL

There are some conditions that are more likely to be missed when you have two children. A hearing problem, for example, often presents with a child being very self-contained and happy to be left to her own devices. This is a relief for most mothers with two young children, and the condition can be overlooked.

Likewise, social problems such as autism can be blamed on an elder child being jealous of their new sibling and so acting up. Again, this can sometimes be missed initially. Even the run-up to a cold or teething can make children bad-tempered and clingy for a few days – and it's very easy to blame such behaviour on the birth of a new sibling rather than administering a bit of TLC and Calpol.

It's sometimes other people in the family, or close friends, who will notice a problem before the parents, especially if they don't see the child every day and are therefore more likely to notice a change. So if someone starts dropping 'hints' about your child's welfare, don't dismiss that person as a busybody straight away. Do keep an open mind and listen to what they are saying, however upsetting it may be.

BED-WETTING

A common response to a new sibling is wetting the bed, even if your child hasn't previously done so. This is most likely to occur in the weeks and months before the arrival of the new baby, and often stops soon after the baby is born and the anticipation and worry ends. This is generally nothing to worry about, although occasionally bed-wetting can mask a medical condition such as a urinary tract infection – in which case your child may also be having accidents during the day, perhaps have pain on urination, fishy-smelling wee, frequent wees, and only wees a little at a time. Bed-wetting can also be an indication of diabetes. Other symptoms again include frequent wees and accidents during the day, as well as being very thirsty and seeming generally unwell and lethargic.

CONSTIPATION

The stress of a new baby arriving causes some children to become constipated and hold on to their stools. Part of the reason is that going to the toilet is one of the few things young children can control – everything else in their lives, including the arrival of their new sibling, is out of their control.

Constipation needs to be resolved quickly, because if it goes on then your child's poos will become dry and hard and painful to pass, which perpetuates the problem.

See your GP if your child seems to have stopped pooing for several days and this isn't his usual pattern. Your doctor may prescribe laxatives or stool-softeners. You can also ensure that your child drinks plenty, and include more fibre in his diet – do this gradually to avoid causing bloating and tummy ache.

WORMS AND NITS

With conditions such as thread worms and nits, you need to treat the entire family as a matter of routine. Thread worms are at least very straightforward to treat – if someone in the family complains of a very, very itchy bottom at bedtime (the worms lay their eggs in the evening) you can buy a family pack of threadworm tablets from the pharmacy then all take one on the same day – check the minimum age. Hand-washing and short nails can be used as a preventative measure to reduce the spread of threadworms.

With lice and nits (the lice eggs), you also have to treat the entire family. The silicone-based treatments are the best option as they don't smell or sting, and work by suffocating the lice. But you still have to comb through everyone's hair to remove the nits, so allow 20 minutes per child, and of course time for you and your partner to treat yourselves. There are no shortcuts with nits – you need to put the hours in with a nit comb if you want to get rid of them.

DISABLED AND CHRONICALLY ILL KIDS

The stress of having a disabled or chronically ill child is immense. You'll spend hours agonizing and worrying about them, desperate to get the best medical care.

It's very easy to overlook the effect this has on your other child. In many families the healthy child gets labelled as the 'easy' one and is constantly praised for being so good and sensible. What's actually happening is that they are expected to be less demanding to compensate for the stress caused by their sibling's illness or condition. This can have a terrible impact, making them feel less loved, less important and also resentful of their sibling.

It's important to meet your healthy child's needs by spending one-to-one time with her. Try to be especially nurturing with your healthy child – she'll see you being very gentle with her sibling and will want the same. Be patient when her needs seem badly timed and trivial – for example, 'Where's my ballet skirt?' when you've just heard disappointing medical test results. And keep explaining what's going on, however young she is. If you shield children from the 'terrible truth', they'll often imagine their own version which will be far more frightening.

By paying plenty of attention to your healthy child, you'll not only boost her confidence and make her happier, but you'll also encourage her to grow up to become caring, mature and accepting of people's differences. Most importantly, she'll find it easier to get on with her sick or disabled sibling as she won't feel so resentful. This will also benefit your sick child, because siblings of sick kids are very good at treating their brother or sister like anyone else, which is very important for a disabled child. Also your disabled or sick child will meet and get to know his sibling's friends and so feel less isolated.

Your healthy child will be horrid to her brother or sister on some days, but this is fine. You deal with it just as you would if both kids were healthy. It's part of growing up together and developing a sibling bond that will hopefully last a lifetime.

CHAPTER 13
Age Gaps

Timing when we have our children isn't generally an exact science. So you may well end up with unexpected age gaps between your children. For example, if you had problems getting pregnant then this will not only mean a delayed start to family life but may also mean a large age gap between your children. On the other hand, not getting pregnant instantly first time around often means that you start trying for a second baby quite quickly and end up with closely spaced children. And happy accidents can also result in close age gaps. Other factors that can result in large age gaps include having to cope with bereavement and illness, and so choosing to delay getting pregnant with your second child. Or perhaps you found having your first baby traumatic so decide to wait a while before getting pregnant again.

Whatever the age difference between your children, there are plenty of advantages and also a few disadvantages. And should you ever find yourself wishing that things had turned out differently, just remember that there's no way on earth that you'd have ended up with the children you have today – it's a biological impossibility. And, thankfully, most of us don't want to trade in our children, even on a bad day.

TINY GAP: 9–18 MONTHS

Pros

Your children will grow up together enjoying similar activities, toys and even television programmes. They'll be very close, have enormous amounts of fun and you'll never have to think of ways to encourage them to play more together. On family outings it will be easy to please both children. And a very small age gap is even thought to produce less sibling jealousy.

Another advantage is that the exhausting early years will be over and done with quickly – so nappies, broken nights and messy meals will soon become a distant memory. In the early years both your children will have an afternoon nap, so you'll get a break during the day, and they'll both have the same bedtime. And if you work you will be on maternity leave while your eldest is still very much a baby, so you'll be around for important milestones such as his first steps and words. You may save on childcare because you could get a nanny for both children – this can work out cheaper than two nursery places.

Finally, you won't have to store masses of stuff because hand-me-down clothes and equipment will go straight to the baby sibling as soon as your eldest is ready to pass them on.

Cons

The closer the gap the more exhausting life is initially as you'll effectively be looking after two babies. Both children will be in nappies and will need carrying, dressing and feeding. Your eldest will still be waking up at night from time to time, and will be mobile so will need constant watching.

You won't always be able to save money with hand-me-downs, for example you may have to buy two cots, high chairs and baby car seats. And from around the time your youngest is 4 months old, you may end up with two children teething at the same time.

MEDIUM GAP: 18 MONTHS–4 YEARS

Pros

Your children will still be close enough in age to want to play with each other, and will enjoy many of the same toys, activities and outings together. But the gap will be big enough to enjoy early milestones with your eldest before the baby is born – for example walking and talking.

Life won't be as exhausting when your baby arrives – you'll feel you have a baby and toddler rather than two babies. Your eldest may even be out of nappies and able to do things for himself, such as getting dressed, and will be competent at feeding himself. And he'll be old enough to understand about the new baby coming, and for you to reassure him that you still love him.

Again, both your children may nap at the same time until your eldest reaches about 3, and they will both have the same bedtime and go to bed early – giving you long evenings to yourselves.

Cons

You'll have to juggle a new baby with a toddler or pre-schooler. Children of this age are likely to be jealous of a new baby and can become particularly angry when you breastfeed or rock a crying baby in your arms. To make matters worse, your toddler will be going through the tantrumming stage and starting to have attitude. As your children grow older, sibling jealousy may be more intense than with a smaller or larger age gap.

LARGER AGE GAP: 4 YEARS OR MORE

Pros

Having a new baby may feel particularly special and exciting after all those years. You'll have the luxury of being on your own with your baby for much of the day and yet you'll be far more competent than first time around.

You'll also have the chance to rest during the day, so are unlikely to become too exhausted.

It's easy to have one-to-one time with each child – you'll play with your baby all day, then switch your focus to your eldest when he gets back from school. Bedtime will be relatively easy – your baby will go to bed first, giving you special one-to-one time with your eldest each evening. With a wide age gap you'll feel less pressured and more able to indulge each of your children. You're unlikely to find having two children any more exhausting than having a baby for the first time – in fact, you may find it easier now that you're an experienced parent. Your eldest may well find having a new baby sibling very exciting and really enjoy being involved and helping out – some children turn out to be incredibly helpful with a new baby. In years to come your younger child will probably greatly admire her older sibling, and he'll feel proud of his role as a much older sibling. He may also enjoy the responsibility of being put in charge of his younger sibling (this must never be forced, however, as it can lead to resentment).

Cons

You may feel daunted by looking after a newborn and feel you've forgotten a lot. Childcare advice is always changing, for example weaning recommendations and vaccination schedules can change every few years.

Returning to round-the-clock feeding and nappy-changing as well as sleepless nights can be a shock if you've left that stage behind once before.

Your older child may feel resentful that life changes so much with a new baby and it's no longer so easy to go out and have fun. And your children are less likely to be playmates, especially if the gap is bigger than 6 years.

You may find yourself mourning your eldest child's babyhood and toddler days – he'll suddenly seem very grown-up and you'll have wistful memories of when he was a chubby little 1-year-old toddling along. Such feelings are common and normal – watching our children grow up is an inevitable part of the bittersweetness of being a parent.

THE PERFECT AGE GAP

From a biological point of view, the perfect age gap is to leave between 18 and 59 months between pregnancies. This means your children will have an age gap of between 2 years 3 months and 4 years 11 months between them.

If you stick to this age gap you'll reduce the risk of premature birth and low birth weight by at least 20 per cent. This data comes from research published in the *Journal of the American Medical Association*, which looked at 67 previous studies covering over 11 million pregnancies from across the world.

The researchers think that having a very short interval between pregnancies, particularly if it's less than 6 months, means that the mother's body doesn't get enough time to recover from the physiological demands of pregnancy, birth and breastfeeding. And a very long gap can result in the gradual decline in the capacity of the mother's body to cope with the demands of pregnancy, so her body will respond as it would have done for her first pregnancy – with similar risks. But not smoking and being generally healthy during your pregnancy will certainly help to reduce such risks.

CHAPTER 14
Are You Going to Have Any More?

This is the question that people often ask once your youngest is walking and talking, and you and your partner are sleeping through the night again. It's also a question we ask ourselves, however many children we have – what would it be like to have just one more? So whether or not you go on to have a third child, it's bound to be something you consider, however briefly.

Having had two children, you'll already know the joy of discovering just how different their characters can be. But as well as enjoying another unique little person in your life, a third child will give your family a whole new dynamic.

For a start, families of three or more children are considered 'big' these days – you're no longer average. And if you've got two boys or two girls, there's the prospect of having a child of the opposite sex – it is especially exciting, once you've become 'used' to having either boys or girls, suddenly to get something different.

But never make this your reason for having another child. Of course it's natural to long secretly for a girl or boy, but try telling yourself that you're going to end up with either three girls or three boys, then see if you still want to go ahead and have another child. We suggest not finding out the sex of your baby at the 5-month scan. It's far more disappointing to discover that your baby is the 'wrong' sex at the scan than to find out while holding him or her in your arms for the first time.

Having more than two children makes the relationships between them more varied. When you have two children, you create one relationship between them. When you have three children, you create three relationships – the relationship between the oldest and middle, the relationship between the middle and youngest, and the relationship between the oldest and the youngest. And when you have four children you create six relationships. Lots of parents of three or more say the rivalry between their children is less intense than in families with two children.

But don't be under any illusions that having three children suddenly makes life easier. Of course it's harder work than having two, but not as hard as you might think. For a start, it's less of a jolt for your other children when a third baby arrives, because they're already used to sharing Mum and Dad. It's also less of a jolt for parents – having had two children, you'll already be used to life revolving around them and getting very little time to yourselves. You'll also be better parents as you've had a fair bit of practice.

As for the baby, third babies have a reputation for being incredibly easy as they simply have to fit in with the family. In some ways she'll be rather under-indulged and will have to get used to waiting to be picked up or fed. But in other ways she'll be incredibly indulged because, as well as her parents, she'll have two older siblings to fuss over her and keep her amused.

And the jump from one to two children is certainly bigger than the jump from two to three – it's double the number of children when you have a second child, compared with the jump going up by just a third when you have your third. And going from three to four children means the jump goes up by just a quarter. Plenty of parents from families of four or more claim that, once you have four, an extra baby makes very little difference to the everyday chaos you are already living in.

With three or more children, life certainly becomes a lot noisier and out of control – you've got more children than hands. But most parents will agree that it's wonderful. Christmas is magical with a house full of excited children, and occasions such as Halloween, Bonfire Night and birthdays are busy and festive with three or more kids – you won't have to invite other children over to make up numbers. Likewise with family days out, or just a trip to your local park, you're a self-contained unit – there's enough of you to have plenty of fun.

Other advantages of a large family are that your children learn from each other – young kids from large families tend to be developmentally quite advanced for their age. And then there's the matter of healthy neglect. Children from large families soon learn to pack their own PE kits and change the batteries in their own toys. When they ask you to do these non-essential tasks, you'll no doubt promise 'in a minute' then never get around to it, as there's always a bottom to wipe or a fight to break up.

When deciding whether or not to have another child, you're bound to consider the 'what ifs' – what if there's something wrong with the baby, or what if it's twins. Of course these are possibilities, but if they haven't put you off so far there's little reason to start using them as excuses now. The only exception is if you are in your 40s, in which case you'll need to weigh up the facts carefully before going ahead. We address these points later in this chapter.

Of course there are downsides to having a larger family – you don't get invited out as much, since five or more of you to feed and fit around a table is a lot. Grandparents may well announce that they're 'happy to take just one child', which is easier for them but doesn't give you much of a break. There's no getting away from the fact that modern life is geared around families of four. For example, 'family tickets' for museums, attractions, theme parks and events are usually for four – you pay extra when you've got more children. Similarly, 'family rooms' in hotels or ferries are usually for four – you'll need to take your own blow-up kids' beds for any extra children. And cafes and restaurants have plenty of tables for four, but larger families may well have to wait.

Cars can also be an issue – most cars can fit two child seats or booster seats on the back seat, but you'll need a larger car to fit three children in their appropriate seats safely across the back. If you've got four or five children, you'll probably need a seven-seater car to take the whole family out. Every child needs to sit securely and safely in the car – squeezing children in without the appropriate seating is not only illegal but dangerous in the event of an accident, even for short trips. The only real way of checking whether a particular car – one you've got or hope to buy – will take three seats abreast is to physically try it out in the car. Don't just rely on dimensions alone, as some car rear seats may have seat cushions or seatbelt fixings that make three child seats impossible to fit.

One option if you have three or more children is a Multimac seat – special seats that combine three or four child places in one continuous seat. These aren't cheap but their design means that you can fit three – or four – children abreast in the back of a smaller or medium-sized vehicle, which may mean you can keep your existing car.

There are many reasons for not having any more children – money, your age, your career, not having enough space or a big enough car, not wanting to be pregnant again, not wanting to give birth again, or not wanting to look after a newborn and be sleep-deprived again.

As a general observation, when you give away your baby stuff, you've stopped. But if it's still in your loft, there's a very good chance you've still got the desire and you'll be having another baby at some point … enjoy!

As for us, the authors, we're both mothers of three and would have loved to have gone on and had more – but we've given away our baby stuff now, so it's not going to happen! We sincerely hope that after reading this book you never consider 'not being able to cope' as a reason for not having more children.

THE 'WHAT IFS'

What If There's Something Wrong with My Baby?

It's very common for women who are pregnant for the third time to worry that something will be wrong their baby. It's an almost superstitious worry; you think you've had two healthy children so surely your luck will have run out. Statistically the odds of having a healthy baby aren't affected by the fact that you've had two children already. In fact, if you've had two healthy children it suggests that you and your partner aren't carriers of genes likely to cause birth defects.

But age can work against you when it comes to having healthy babies. Your risk of having a baby with chromosomal abnormalities increases with age. And Down's syndrome is the most common chromosomal birth defect.

Down Syndrome Risk

The risk of having a baby with Down Syndrome increases with the age of the mother, as shown below:

- Age 30 – 1 in 1,000
- Age 35 – 1 in 400
- Age 40 – 1 in 100
- Age 45 – 1 in 30

In the majority of birth defects the cause is unclear but it is thought to be due to an interplay of environmental and genetic factors. By avoiding drugs, medicines, alcohol and smoking during pregnancy, and taking folic acid and being generally healthy, it is possible to reduce the risk of having an abnormal baby.

What If It's Twins?

The first thing you may ask at your scan is, 'is it twins?', because you dread not being able to cope. Statistically the chance is 98.5 per cent that you will be having just one baby. This reduces slightly to 97.8 per cent if you are over 35.

Other factors that increase your chances of having twins include:

- taking fertility drugs or having fertility treatment
- if you are a twin or your mother is – this means you may carry a gene for hyper-ovulation and release more than one egg per cycle.
- if you have had twins already
- if you are obese
- if you are very tall
- if you are Afro-Caribbean (Asian and Hispanic women are the least likely to give birth to twins).

CHAPTER 15
Routine

Here's an at-a-glance guide to how much sleep and food your children need at different ages. We hope that having this information to hand will help you to organize your family into a routine, and also to adapt your routine as your children get older.

Do note that this is just a guide; if you try to stick to it closely you will probably become very frustrated. Any number of events can blow apart a sleeping and feeding routine including illness, teething and life events such as moving house or simply a night away.

It's normal for broken nights to happen from time to time until your child is at least 5, and for fussy eating to occur often until about the age of 6 or older. But you'll see from our tables that naps and milk feeds soon get dropped, so after the age of 3 the only 'routine' your children require is 3 meals a day and an early night. Of course you'll still need to play with your children and take them out regularly for exercise and fun, but life will become unrecognizably flexible compared with the early days of coping with two!

SLEEP

1 month – up to 17 hours of sleep needed

- No sleep pattern, lots of mini-naps, awake in the evenings.

2 months – up to 17 hours of sleep needed

- May sleep for a long spell during the night, up to 5 hours.
- You can aim for 3 naps a day: morning, long lunchtime nap, late afternoon nap.
- Probably awake in the evenings.
- Will need to go into a cot at about 10 weeks because too big for her Moses basket.

3 months – up to 16 hours of sleep needed

- May sleep for 5 hours or more during the night.
- May nap 3 times a day for a total of 3 hours or more.
- Your baby will start to go to bed early and you can establish a bedtime routine.

4 months – up to 16 hours of sleep needed

- Physically capable of sleeping for up to 8 hours during the night uninterrupted and without milk. Try not to feed more than once during the night.
- May still wake up to 4 times a night.
- Daytime napping pattern will become more defined – 2 short naps 30–40 minutes, and a longer lunchtime nap 2–3 hours.

5 months – 14½ to 15½ hours of sleep needed

- Aim for an early night and 8 hours' uninterrupted sleep during the night.
- May drop late afternoon nap.

6 months – 14 to 15 hours of sleep needed

- Physically capable of sleeping for up to 12 hours at night uninterrupted and without milk. But 8 hours is very acceptable at this age.
- 2 to 3 daytime naps totalling 3 hours or more including a long 2-hour lunchtime nap.
- Drop the night-feed if you haven't already done so.
- Your baby can go into her own room.

7 months – 14 to 15 hours of sleep needed

- Sleeping for 8–12 hours uninterrupted at night.
- 2 naps – morning and lunchtime – the lunchtime nap will be longer once your baby has dropped her late afternoon nap, between 2 and 3 hours long.

8 months – 14 to 15 hours of sleep needed

- Sleeping for 8–12 hours uninterrupted at night.
- 2 naps.
- May roll onto her front to sleep.

9 to 10 months – 14 to 15 hours of sleep needed

- Sleeping for 9–12 hours uninterrupted at night.
- 1 or 2 naps – some babies will drop their morning nap around now, others will continue having 2 naps a day until about 18 months.

- Babies develop attitude around now and some will become angry about being put down for a nap. Your baby may like to have a comfort toy at night from this age.

- Lower the cot mattress because your baby will soon be standing.

11 to 12 months – 14 to 15 hours of sleep needed

- Sleeping for 10–12 hours uninterrupted at night.

- 1 or 2 naps.

- Use a quilt instead of a baby-sleeping bag once your baby is able to stand.

13 to 16 months – 13½ to 14½ hours of sleep needed

- Sleeping for 11–12 hours uninterrupted at night.

- 1 or 2 naps. If she still has her morning nap it will become shorter – perhaps just 30 minutes.

- Your baby may fuss when you leave the room because separation anxiety peaks.

17 to 20 months – 13 to 14 hours of sleep needed

- Sleeping for 11–12 hours uninterrupted at night.

- 1 lunchtime nap – 1½ to 2 hours (most toddlers drop their morning nap by about 17 months).

- Toddlers who are 91cm (3ft) tall will need a 'big' bed – they are tall enough to vault out of their cots. May start using delaying tactics at bedtime such as that he wants another story, a drink or a clean nappy.

21 to 24 months – 12½ to 13½ hours of sleep needed

- Sleeping for 11–12 hours uninterrupted at night.
- 1 lunchtime nap – 1 to 1½ hours

2 to 2½ years – 12 to 13 hours of sleep needed

- Sleeping for 11–12 hours uninterrupted at night.
- 1 lunchtime nap – no more than 1½ hours or night sleep may be affected.
- Can start to become afraid of the dark. May start to enjoy his afternoon nap and perhaps even ask to be put to bed sometimes.

2½ to 3 years – 11½ to 12½ hours of sleep needed

- Sleeping for 11–12 hours uninterrupted at night.
- Between the ages of 2 and 3 toddlers drop their lunchtime nap so will either have quiet time or just a short 45-minute nap.
- May learn to climb out of the cot between the ages of 2 and 3. This is the age when children can start to get over-excited and play up at bedtime, especially if they have siblings to collude with. It can be tremendous fun goading their parents.

3 years – 11 to 12 hours of sleep needed

- Sleeping for 11–12 hours uninterrupted at night.
- Will drop lunchtime nap, although may still sleep in the car or buggy during the day. Nightmares can become a problem by the age of 3 and children can suffer badly for a few months. This is also the age when some children can stay dry at night and come out of nappies, but lots aren't ready until later.

4 years – 11 to 12 hours of sleep needed

- Most children grow out of bed-wetting by around now.

5 to 12 years – 10 to 11 hours of sleep needed

- Most children grow out of nightmares by the age of 5.
- Seek medical help if your child is still wetting the bed at 7.

12 – 18 years – 8½ to 10 hours of sleep needed

- Due to hormonal changes, teenagers' internal body clocks sometimes alter making it harder for them to go to bed early, so a lie-in becomes inevitable.

18+ years – 7½ to 9 hours of sleep needed

- Adults generally need less sleep than teens because they aren't growing.
- Some adults seem to need far less sleep than this.

FEEDING

Please note that fluid ounces and pints are given in US measures.

1 week

- Up to 12 milk feeds a day.
- Up to 600ml (1¼ pints), a maximum of 90ml (3fl.oz) in one feed.
- Growth spurt at 3 weeks.

1 month

- Up to 10 milk feeds a day.
- Up to 750ml (1½ pints), a maximum of 120ml (4fl.oz) in one feed.
- Growth spurt at 6 weeks.

2 months

- Up to 9 milk feeds a day.
- Up to 960ml (2 pints), a maximum of 180ml (6fl.oz) in one feed.

3 months

- Up to 8 milk feeds a day.
- Up to 1.2ltrs (2½ pints), a maximum of 210ml (7fl.oz) in one feed.
- Growth spurt at 12 weeks.

4 months

- Up to 7 milk feeds a day.
- Up to 1.2ltrs (2½ pints), a maximum of 240ml (8fl.oz) in one feed.

5 months

- Up to 6 milk feeds a day.
- Up to 1.2ltrs (2½ pints) a day, a maximum of 240ml (8fl.oz) in one feed.

6 months

- Up to 5 milk feeds a day.
- Weaning begins with a few mouthfuls of puree and finger foods once a day, and after 2 weeks your baby should be eating solids twice a day. Gradually increase this to 3 times a day. Include a couple of iron-rich foods a day such as meat, eggs, lentils, green vegetables and mashed breakfast cereals (fortified with iron).
- Easy finger foods: broccoli, banana, toast, sticks of cheese and a large chunk of meat to suck.

7 months

- 3 to 5 milk feeds a day, but no milk during the night.

- 2–3 solid meals a day, including iron-rich foods and lumpy food.

- Mashed foods that aren't so smooth to introduce your baby to lumps: mashed potato, sweet potato, avocado and peach.

8 months

- 3 or 4 milk feeds a day reducing to just 3 a day by the end of the month.

- 2–3 solid meals a day.

- Lumpier foods that are harder to swallow: rice, pasta shapes, grated cheese, bread.

9 months

- A pint of formula milk or breast milk in either 2 large feeds or 3 smaller ones.

- Your baby should be eating 3 solid meals a day by now including:
  - 3–4 servings of carbohydrates (bread, rice, pasta, potatoes)
  - 3–4 servings of fruit and vegetables
  - 2 servings of protein (meat, fish, eggs, cheese, yoghurt)
  - Optional – 2 small healthy snacks such as fruit, toast or a handful of dried cereal (a good source of iron).

- Include lots of finger food now that your baby is more dexterous, including tiny food that she can pick up with her fingers: peas, blueberries cut in half, raisins, raw carrot batons, meat cut into tiny pieces.

1 year

- No more formula milk; you can use full fat cow's milk instead but ideally give it to your baby in a cup not a bottle as this is better for teeth. She can have 400ml a day (just under a pint) including what she has on her cereal and so on. This gives her plenty of calcium without filling her up so much that she doesn't eat solid food. Your toddler should only be given milk or water to drink to minimize tooth decay.

- Your baby is now allowed to eat:
    o Honey – this can cause botulism in the under-1s
    o Eggs that are soft boiled, fried or poached (up until now your baby was only allowed hard-boiled or scrambled eggs to reduce the risk of food poisoning).

- Your baby can feed herself with a spoon (it will be messy for at least 3 months) and drink from a cup with no lid.

- She will need feeding punctually to avoid frustrated tantrums when she gets hungry.

15 months

- Fussiness can begin and your toddler may only want to eat familiar foods. And she will become aware of treats, realizing that some foods (such as ice-cream) taste nicer than others.

18 months

- Iron deficiency can show up if your baby has been drinking too much milk and not enough iron-rich solid food. Symptoms include pale lower eyelids and lack of appetite.

2 years

- Your toddler can have semi-skimmed milk instead of full fat – this is just as rich in calcium.
- Increase your toddler's fruit and vegetable intake from 3 to 5 portions a day – portions are much smaller than an adult's – a quarter of a peach, 5 green beans, a dessert spoon of baked beans and a small handful of raisins all count as a portion.

3 years

- Your child's tummy is still small so he shouldn't eat too many fibre-rich foods because these will fill him up and possibly stop him from getting enough calories and nutrients.

4 years

- Your child can gradually move towards eating more fibre (whole grains, brown rice, brown pasta and dried fruit) and foods that are lower in fat.

5 years+

- Your child is now allowed to eat whole nuts, cherries and whole grapes because the risk of choking is now greatly reduced. And he is old enough to drink skimmed milk, but this isn't essential – semi-skimmed is fine if this is what the rest of the family drinks.
- Just as adults should aim at eating low-fat, low-salt, low-sugar, high-fibre diets, the over-5s also need to aim at these healthy guidelines.

RESOURCES

Postnatal Depression Test

www.testandcalc.com/etc/tests/edin.asp

www.mind.org

Car Seats

The consumers' group Which? has an updated list of best-buy car seats – www.which.co.uk

www.multimac.co.uk

RoSPA Child Car Seats – A site backed by the Royal Society for the Prevention of Accidents, with full details on choosing, fitting and using child car seats – as well as the laws on carrying children in countries across the world – www.childcarseats.org.uk

ACKNOWLEDGEMENTS

We would like to thank Paul Johnson and Jude Cave for all their help and ideas. We'd also like to thank Maxine Phelops and Nicole Horwitz at Whittington Health for their invaluable input. Finally we'd like to say a special thank you to the team at Hay House, especially Carolyn Thorne, Julie Oughton, Jessica Crockett and Leanne Siu Anatasi. And last but not least our agent Barbara Levy for her constant support and encouragement.

INDEX

This index is arranged in word-by-word alphabetical order.

A

A&E, when to go 175, 176, 177–9
accidents 182–4
after-school clubs 94, 135, 145
age gaps 121, 189–93
aggression 125, 137, 148, 164–5, 170
    (*see also* fights)
ambulances, calling 179
antibiotics 42, 175
attention-seeking behaviour 36, 65,
    78–9, 106, 161, 163 (*see also*
    one-to-one time; protest pooing;
    regression)
autism 185

B

baby blues 40
baby-proofing 24, 117, 184
bath, first 43–4
bathtime
    involving sibling 43–4, 45, 92–3
    routines 61–2, 67, 69–70, 77, 127

safety 24, 69, 139–40
    willy-pulling/touching bits 130
bedtime routines 8–9, 13–14, 69–70,
    127–8, 202
    staggering 128, 145, 192
    synchronizing 60, 103, 128, 148
bed-wetting 186, 205
bending 18
bibs 62, 94
bickering 161, 163
'big bed,' transferring to 7, 204
birth
    preparations 3–4, 18–20, 22–3,
        25–6
    recovery 32–3, 40
birth defects 199
biting 137–8, 162
bladder, leaky 115
blanket, 'our snuggle' 21–2
bonding (*see also* one-to-one time)
    father-baby 86
    mother-child 21–2, 29, 40, 43, 153
    sibling 47, 105, 119, 147, 188

booster seats 122, 198
boredom 38, 81, 87, 160, 179
bottle-feeding 33, 42, 113, 115, 136
    preparing kit 13
    obesity link 175
    regression 79
    sections to read xi
    by sibling 76
bouncy chairs 61, 62, 63, 67, 69, 118
Braxton Hicks contractions 20
breakfast routine 8, 63, 136
breastfeeding (see also night-feeds;
        weaning)
    choking on milk 38
    distraction during 89–90
    entertaining your toddler 53–4, 67
    giving up 14, 15, 33–4, 136
    guilt 42
    kit 13
    mastitis 41–2, 89
    mimicking with toys 80, 92
    patterns 40, 69, 74, 76, 101, 115
    sore nipples 13–14, 41, 89
    taking medication 32
    tandem-feeding 14–15
bringing baby home 31–2, 35–6
buggies
    burning calories 114
    double 11–12, 58, 88, 102
    at the park 118–19, 141
    routines 58, 63, 90, 96, 107
    walking with toddler 56, 78, 88
buggy boards 12
building games 119, 138, 143, 169
bullying 162, 164–6
bunk beds 146

C

Caesareans 3–4, 19, 32, 115
calcium needs 136, 209
calories, burning 114
Calpol 174, 177, 181–2
car journeys 96–7, 184
car seats 184, 190, 198, 211
carriers 88, 96, 109, 119 (see also slings)
chasing games 138
chickenpox 174, 175, 176
Child Benefit 84
childcare 10, 72–3, 75, 83–4
    during birth 20, 21, 25–6
    costs 135, 190
choking hazards 76, 119, 122, 124,
        183, 210
chores, involving toddler 47, 125
chronic illnesses 187–8
cleaners 24, 26, 73, 83
cleaning shortcuts 96
climbing 7, 54, 117, 146, 205
clingy behaviour 64, 137, 185
clothes (see also laundry)
    nappy access 62–3, 82
    sibling rivalry 159
colds 34–5, 174, 176, 185
colic 76, 79–80, 89, 90
collusion 46, 69, 81, 205
colostrum 14, 33, 34
colour schemes 147
comparing children 140, 153–4, 155,
        187
computer games 94, 124–5
constipation 32, 186
contractions 20–1
cooking
    playtime 95, 119, 120

shortcuts 2, 67, 83, 95, 107–9, 128–9
copycat phase *see* hero-worship
cord stumps 44
cot death 12, 66, 77
cots 12, 69, 104, 190, 202
  growing out of 7, 203, 204, 205
cow's milk 122, 136, 208, 209, 210
crawling 117, 118, 119, 123
crèche services 114
crying 76, 77, 90, 144
  both at once 65–6, 84–5, 96, 130
  explaining to toddler 22, 46, 80, 81
cuddles 16, 21, 64, 78, 110
cups, drinking from 129, 137, 208, 209
cuts 177, 178

D

Dads
  advice for xi, 75
  father-baby bond 86
darkness, being afraid 147, 205
dehydration 35, 174–5, 176, 186
diabetes 186
diarrhoea 174, 176
diary dates 49
disabled children 187–8
doctors
  playing 119
  telephone appointments 175–6, 178
  when to consult 42, 101, 115, 149, 176, 186, 205
Down's Syndrome 199
dressing 6–7, 18, 61–2, 158

E

eggs, food poisoning risk 122, 209
elbow injuries 183
emotional responses 1, 11, 32–3, 110, 155–6, 162
epidurals 4, 19
Ergo baby carrier 12, 88
exercise 88–9, 114–15 (*see also* pelvic floor exercises)
exhaustion 60, 72, 85, 110, 148

F

fair, being 159–60, 169, 181
falls 177–8, 183
family size 200
father-baby bond 86
favouritism 46, 89, 152–3, 160, 181
feeding (*see also* bottle-feeding; breastfeeding)
  calcium needs 136, 209
  choking 38, 76, 122, 124, 210
  demand 42, 74, 76, 99
  dietary fibre 186, 210
  distraction during 89–90
  fussy eating 2, 14, 95, 140, 201, 209
  growth spurts 55, 74, 89, 101, 206, 207
  holding cutlery 6, 137, 209
  iron needs 122, 207, 208, 209
  at mealtimes 63, 65, 68
  night-feeds 99, 101–2, 113, 203
  patterns 9, 55, 97, 103–4, 206–10
  portion sizes 209–10
  preparing kit 13
  sick children 174–5
  tandem-feeding 14
  weaning 14–15, 115, 192, 207–9

fevers 176, 177, 181

fibre intake 186, 210

fights
coping strategies 161–6, 167–71
reasons for 152, 160–1
saying 'sorry' 166–7, 170

finger foods 109, 122, 124, 207, 208

fire risks 185

formula milk 13, 42, 115, 208

fractures 177–8

friends, help from 49, 73–4, 89, 125, 185

frozen meals 26–7, 68, 95

fruit, eating 129, 208, 209, 210

fussy eating 2, 14, 95, 140, 201, 209

G

games 81, 85–6, 119, 138–9, 143

gardens 85–6

genitals
naming 43–4
sibling curiosity 43, 130

getting up 9, 60–1

gifts
from baby 23, 27, 36
fairness 159
for new baby 44–5

grandparents xi, 10, 25, 49–50, 89, 197

growth spurts (baby) 55, 74, 89, 90, 101, 206, 207

guilt 14, 37, 42, 148–9, 151

H

hands, cleaning 34, 176

hatred
elder for sibling 78, 80, 110, 155–6, 165

feeling for your children 148–9

head injuries 178, 183

hearing problems 185

help
asking for 24, 33, 57, 72–3, 149
from family 25, 47–9, 49–50, 116, 185 (see also grandparents)

hero-worship 136–7, 142, 154, 192

hide and seek 138

high chairs 9, 18, 122, 140, 190

holidays 103, 197

home births 18, 19, 22, 25, 31, 32

homework battles 93–4

honey 209

hospital bag 18, 27

housekeeping
accepting mess 37–8, 83, 121
early days 37–8, 47–9, 58
help from visitors 47–9, 73
night routines 60
playing with toddler 47, 125
during pregnancy 11–13, 24–8
shortcuts 94–6, 107–9, 128–9

humour, using 167, 168

hunger, and irritability 57, 160, 209

hypno-birthing 3

I

ibuprofen 174, 177, 181–2

identity, developing own 140, 154–5

illness and injury
accidents 182–4
chronic 187–8
coping strategies 174–5, 178–9, 180–2
not noticing 185
seeking help 175–6, 177–9

immune system 33, 174, 176, 177

immunizations 88, 100, 134, 192
impulse control 170
independence, teaching 6–7
iron needs 122, 207, 208, 209
ironing shortcuts 95
isolation 148

J

jealousy (*see also* sibling rivalry)
  elder child's 46, 106, 126, 180–1
  helpful strategies 155–60
  primal response 137, 151
  toddler's 55, 78, 91–2, 104–5, 123,
    191
jigsaws 139
judgemental mums 130–1

K

kitchen timer 68, 85, 92

L

labelling children 154–5, 187
labour 3–4, 18–19, 20–1
  explaining to toddlers 22–3, 25
language development, delayed 142
laughing 102, 104, 106
laundry 13, 24, 48, 73, 94–5
leaving the house, routines 9, 57,
    58–9, 63–4, 96–7
lice 187
lifting (*see also* slings), physical
    demand 15–16, 88
lighting 147
lips, split 177
listening 56, 158, 164, 165, 167
lock-up boxes 146
lumpy foods 122, 207, 208
lunchtime

naps 91, 121, 202, 203, 204, 205
  routine 8, 65–6

M

makeup, making time for 62
manual dexterity 124, 126, 208, 209
marriage problems 116
mashed foods 107, 122, 128, 207,
    208
mastitis 41–2, 89
maternity nurses 26
mattresses 12, 34, 203
mealtime tips 2, 68–9, 72, 122,
    128–9 (*see also* feeding, patterns;
    regression)
medicines 174, 175, 180, 181–2, 186
midwives 3, 19, 21, 33
milestones
  sibling reaction 91–2, 93, 123, 126,
    133
  timings 7, 113, 117, 142
milk, cow's 122, 136, 208, 209, 210
milk ducts, blocked 41–2
milk feeds 35, 115, 136, 206, 207,
    208
milk flow 38, 74
misbehaviour, reasons for 28, 48, 64,
    78, 123–4, 126–7
morning sickness 2, 11, 14
Moses baskets 12, 61, 67, 69
daytime naps 42, 44, 66, 78
mothers-in-law 24, 48, 49–50
mucus, clearing passages 34–5
Multimac seats 198
'mummies and daddies,' games
    139
muscle development (baby) 66, 69,
    77, 102, 118

N

nappies, regression 79
nappy changing 18, 42, 62, 63, 76, 80
  dehydration signs 35
  nappy kit 12–13, 42
  'poo chart' game 81
nappy rash 42, 57, 63
naps
  baby's 42, 44, 57, 90–1, 104
  recommended routines 201, 202, 203, 204, 205
  synchronizing 91, 103, 121
  toddler's 8, 56, 66
NHS direct 176
nicknames 155
night-feeds 99, 101–2, 113, 203
nightmares 13, 205
nipples, sore 13, 41, 89
nits 187
noise 35, 43, 55, 144, 184
nursery 11, 56, 125, 135, 190 (see also school runs)

O

one-to-one time
  building into routine 67, 110, 125, 145, 192
  with healthy child 188
  rectifying poor behaviour 36, 81, 105, 106, 111, 123
over-excitement 144, 205

P

pain, womb contraction 32
paracetamol see Calpol
parks see playgrounds

partners
  communication with 24, 75, 116, 181
  eating with 59, 68, 107
  tough times 75, 116
pelvic floor exercises 41, 89, 115
pharmacists, consulting 175, 178, 181
Pilates 89, 115
placid babies 118, 137
play (see also one-to-one time)
  child-led 54, 110
  ideas 67, 119–20, 138–9
  quality attention through 28, 48, 81–3, 92
play dates 147
play dough 120
play-fighting 139, 162, 170–1
playgrounds 118–19, 141, 182–3
playgroups 49, 56, 58, 64–5, 118
playpens 67, 117
'please,' use of 131
postnatal depression 100–1, 211
potty-training 15, 105, 137
praise
  descriptive 36, 78–9, 92, 94, 153
  sibling resentment 65, 123, 154, 187
pregnancy
  announcing and explaining 1, 5–6, 10–11, 22–3
  perfect gaps between 193
  physical impact 2–3, 15–16, 17, 18, 21
  split focus during 29
presents see gifts
pretending games 52, 138, 139
protest pooing 82
punishment 138, 143, 158, 165–6
purees 122, 207

Q

quilts 204

R

race the clock, not each other 158–9
red books 84
registering baby 84
regression 6, 78, 79, 92, 123–4, 126
re-heating foods 107–8, 109
relationships, tough times 75, 116
reward charts 94
risks, learning about 183
road safety 96, 135
roast dinners 108
room-sharing 127–8, 146–8
roundabouts 141
routines
    bathtime and bedtime 8–9, 13–14,
        60, 69–70, 127–8, 202
    feeding 9, 55, 97, 103–4, 206–10
    leaving the house 9, 57, 58–9,
        63–4, 96–7
    napping patterns 90–1, 201–5
    night sleep 35, 99, 113, 201–6
    night-feeds 102, 113, 203
    supermarket trips 109–10
    tips for establishing 8–9, 35, 44, 45,
        78, 99–100

S

sandpits 141
scans 5, 195–6, 200
school 11, 28, 93, 135, 153
    rules for missing 180–1
school runs 53, 56–7, 91
self-esteem 140, 142, 154–5
separation anxiety 137, 204

sharing 138, 146–7, 168–9 (see also
    room-sharing)
shelves, as personal territory 127,
    146–7
shoes in the hall 7
shopping (grocery) 26–7, 73, 83, 95
    supermarket trips 109–10
shops, playing 119
sibling rivalry (see also fights; jealousy)
    comparisons 140, 153–4, 155, 187
    family size 196
    favouritism 46, 89, 152–3
    helpful strategies 155–60
    labels 154–5, 187
    normal instinct 151, 161–2
six-week checks 84
skin conditions, common 175
sleep
    patterns 42–3, 99, 102–3, 113, 201–6
    sleeping position 66–7, 203
    sleeping through 13–14, 202, 203,
        204, 205
    tips for establishing a routine 35,
        44, 55, 78
slings 12, 55, 64, 65, 88
    soothing effect 60, 69, 90, 117
smiling 86, 87, 90, 92, 105
smoke alarms 185
snacks 9, 14, 53, 126, 208
soft balls, rolling 119
solids see weaning
'sorry,' saying 162, 166–7, 170
spoon-feeding 123, 126
spoons, use by baby 6, 123, 137, 209
stealing 157–8
stomach bugs 174, 176
stories
    about new babies 28

reading one-to-one 21, 67, 69, 153, 161
reading to both 120, 139, 147, 148
settling rituals 8, 128
stress, managing your 9, 71, 72, 85, 148–9
supermarket trips 109–10
swings 118–19, 141, 182

T

table manners 9, 126–7
tale-telling 157
tantrums 85, 135, 153, 209
teasing 137, 158, 163–4
teatime routine 68–9
teenagers 206
television 54, 94, 124–5, 136, 168
territory, sense of 53, 146
'thank you,' use of 131
third pregnancies, considering 40, 195–200
threadworms 187
'time-out' rule 170, 171
tiredness
    of Mum see exhaustion
    sibling fights 68, 160, 170
toddlers
    energy levels 85–6, 97
    hurting the baby 36, 110–11, 130, 142–3
    jealousy 55, 78, 91–2, 104–5, 123, 191
touch, bonding through 34, 35, 36, 153 (see also cuddles)
toys
    'baby' kit 54, 80, 92
    bath 61–2, 139
    gift 'from baby' 27

hazards 117, 119, 183
during illness 174, 179
rotating 61, 117
sharing 146–7, 159, 168–9
squabbling over 120, 137, 168–9
territory for special 53, 127, 146
treats 109, 145, 209
tummy time 77, 102
twins 197, 200
two under 2 28, 38, 121, 134–5, 190

V

vaccinations see immunizations
vases 28
vegetables
    cooking 95, 107, 108
    servings 207, 208, 209
visiting 74, 131
visitors 27, 34, 44, 47–9, 96
vomiting 174

W

walks 97, 114, 121
washing see laundry
water births 18
water confidence 139
weaning 14–15, 115, 122, 192, 207–9
willy-pulling/touching bits 130
winding 55, 77, 79–80, 90
wish lists, for partners 116
womb contraction 32
work, returning to 115, 135–6
worms 187

TROUBLESHOOTING INDEX

Here we highlight the issues you may encounter once you have two children. The main index covers some of these problems in greater depth.

attention-seeking behaviour 36, 65, 78–9, 106, 161, 163 (*see also* one-to-one time; protest pooing; regression)

biting 137–8, 162
bonding process 29, 86
boredom of sibling 81, 160
breastfeeding
  choking on milk 38
  distraction during 89–90
  entertaining your toddler 53–4, 67
  giving up 14, 15, 136
  guilt 42
  mastitis 41–2, 89
  sore nipples 13, 41, 89
  tandem-feeding 14–15

car journeys 96-7, 184
colic 76, 79–80, 89, 90
crying, both at once 65, 84–5, 96, 130

exhaustion 61, 72, 85, 102, 110

favouritism 46, 89, 152–3, 160, 181
fussy eating 2, 14, 95, 140, 201, 209

growth spurts (baby) 55, 74, 89, 90, 101, 206, 207

hatred
  eldest for baby 78, 80, 110, 155–6, 165
  for your children 148–9

jealousy
  elder child's 46, 106, 126, 180–1
  helpful strategies 155–60
  toddler's 55, 78, 91–2, 104–5, 123, 191
judgemental mums 130–1

language development, delayed 142
lifting, during pregnancy 15–16

misbehaviour 28, 48, 64, 78, 123–4, 126–7
mothers-in-law 24, 48, 49–50

one-to-one time 67, 110, 125, 145, 192

partners, time together 59, 68, 75, 116
postnatal depression 100–1, 211
potty-training 15, 105, 137
protest pooing 82

regression 6, 63, 78, 79, 92, 123–4, 126
routines
   bathtime and bedtime 8–9, 13–14, 59–60, 68–70, 127–8, 202
   feeding patterns 9, 55, 97, 103–4, 206–10
   leaving the house 9, 57, 58–9, 63, 96–7
   napping patterns 90–1, 201–5

night sleep 35, 99, 113, 201–6
night-feeding 102, 113, 203
supermarket trips 109–10
tips for establishing 8–9, 35, 44, 45, 78, 99–100

sharing 138, 146–7, 168–9
siblings fighting 167–71
supermarket trips 109–10

toddlers
   energy levels 85–6, 97
   hurting the baby 36, 110–11, 130, 142–3
   jealousy 55, 78, 91–2, 104–5, 123, 191
   two under 2 28, 38, 121, 134–5, 190
   willy-pulling/touching bits 130

JOIN THE HAY HOUSE FAMILY

As the leading self-help, mind, body and spirit publisher in the UK, we'd like to welcome you to our family so that you can enjoy all the benefits our website has to offer.

 **EXTRACTS** from a selection of your favourite author titles

 **COMPETITIONS, PRIZES & SPECIAL OFFERS** Win extracts, money off, downloads and so much more

 **LISTEN** to a range of radio interviews and our latest audio publications

 **CELEBRATE YOUR BIRTHDAY** An inspiring gift will be sent your way

 **LATEST NEWS** Keep up with the latest news from and about our authors

 **ATTEND OUR AUTHOR EVENTS** Be the first to hear about our author events

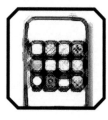 **iPHONE APPS** Download your favourite app for your iPhone

 **HAY HOUSE INFORMATION** Ask us anything, all enquiries answered

join us online at **www.hayhouse.co.uk**

Astley House, 33 Notting Hill Gate
London W11 3JQ
T: 020 3675 2450 E: info@hayhouse.co.uk

ABOUT THE AUTHORS

Simone Cave was the health editor at the *Daily Mirror* for eight years and is now a freelance journalist covering nutrition, health, medical and parenting issues for national newspapers and magazines. Simone also writes books and is the author of five international bestsellers on parenting and childcare. Simone lives with her husband and three children, aged eight, seven and four, in south London.

Dr Caroline Fertleman is Consultant Paediatrician at the Whittington Hospital, London. She also works at the Institute of Child Health at University College London and has an honorary contract at Great Ormond Street Hospital for Children. Caroline has written several books on babies, toddlers and potty training. She lives in London with her husband and three children.

www.yourbabyandchild.com